William Campbell

An Account of Missionary Success in the Island of Formosa

William Campbell

An Account of Missionary Success in the Island of Formosa

ISBN/EAN: 9783744708692

Printed in Europe, USA, Canada, Australia, Japan

Cover: Foto ©ninafisch / pixelio.de

More available books at **www.hansebooks.com**

MISSIONARY SUCCESS

IN THE

ISLAND OF FORMOSA

AN ACCOUNT OF
Missionary Success
IN THE ISLAND OF
FORMOSA

PUBLISHED IN LONDON IN 1650 AND NOW
REPRINTED WITH COPIOUS
APPENDICES

BY

REV. WM. CAMPBELL, F.R.G.S.
ENGLISH PRESBYTERIAN MISSION
TAIWANFOO

IN TWO VOLUMES—VOL. II.

LONDON
TRÜBNER & CO., 57 LUDGATE HILL
1889

XV.

PERSONAL EXPERIENCES OF RECENT
MISSIONARY WORK IN FORMOSA
—*continued.*

BY REV. W. CAMPBELL.

6. *More about the Sek-hoan.*

AMOY, 21 *July* 1874.—I came over here a few days ago to make arrangements for the erection of a mission-house at Taiwanfoo, but it is still possible to furnish some notes regarding my latest visit to our stations in the county of Chiang-hoa. The immediately preceding journey to that region took place during the autumn of last year, when I was accompanied by the English Consul, and by a Mr. Steere from Michigan, who was on the hunt for all sorts of specimens to illustrate the *fauna* and *flora* of the Island. It was the occasion of my second visit to Lake Candidius, and we carried through rather an adventurous expedition among the savages to the east of Po-sia. As, however, full notices of that journey have appeared elsewhere, the following remarks must be confined to the one from which I returned last month.

This spring sojourn in the north extended from 6th April till 6th June, my stay in Po-sia alone lasting for over four weeks. The churches there continue to show signs of spiritual life and progress. The outward boundary has not been much enlarged, our people for the most part being still confined to the three villages in which chapels have been erected. It was my privilege to baptize six adults from the large company of candidates at O-gu-lan, four from those at Gu-khun-soa, and two from the few who were proposed at Toa-to-sia. The difficulty in this part of the work lies chiefly in the fact that we see so little of the inquirers ourselves. I would hope, however, that Khai-san, and another quiet, sensible-looking man who has been chosen to act with him as Elder, may soon be able to render assistance in every such matter.

On the occasion of this visit, we had a very interesting meeting of all the children connected with the three congregations. We met in the chapel at O-gu-lan. There were exactly one hundred present; to whom a liberal supply of refreshments was given, consisting of glutinous rice boiled in brown sugar, hemp-seed cakes, and a sticky sort of Chinese sweetmeat, which was greatly relished. They were much interested while listening to a number of stories about Bible children, but the outstanding feature of our meeting was the hymn-singing. These aborigines have all a greater fondness for music than the Chinese, and we ought certainly to take note of this. I have more than once observed the enlivening effect of distinct, hearty singing at our stations in the Baksa region, and Christians at home are now being taught that the service of song should occupy a very high place in the worship of God.

As two of the native preachers had accompanied me from Taiwanfoo, there happened to be five of them together in Po-sia at this time, and the circumstance was taken advantage of to have a large amount of reading and examination work with them. We found time for going over the greater part of the Acts of the

Apostles, the exercise proving to be most helpful to myself, and not without profit to the others. Our preachers now stationed in Po-sia are:—Brother *Iam* at Gu-khun-soa, doing very well on the whole, especially among the children, in which work he is ably assisted by his intelligent wife; *Ki-chheng* at Toa-lam, whose time at present is occupied chiefly in superintending the erection of the new chapel : and *Ong-lai* at O-gu-lan, who gets another change to the south after doing good service here, his place being taken by one of the young men who came with me, Brother *Kib* from Poah-be.

At Lai-sia, I found matters going on in much the usual way. We wish to see greater prominence given to the educational work here. Preaching and listening to daily remarks on the Scriptures are doubtless of much importance, but without some kind of backbone, so to speak, the people forget what they hear, and have their interest only partially awakened. One young woman was admitted to Church membership on this occasion, but all the other candidates were far back. The two Elders seem to have been taking a warm interest in the welfare of the people, and spent the whole time with me during our prolonged examinations.

To-day, I can well recall the words and gentle character of one of them, named Bun-liong. It was soon after my return to Taiwanfoo that the Lai-sia preacher sent a letter to inform me that this beloved brother had been cruelly murdered by savages. With his little daughter, and an old female fellow-member, he went out one day to dig potatoes, and was fired upon by some persons lying in ambush.

He wheeled round to see his aged companion fall to the ground, and a party of naked savages rushing down to complete their work of destruction. He stood for a moment to defend the child — who escaped into a neighbouring clump of bushes—and then ran towards the village, but while doing so his foot tripped, and he was just in the act of recovering himself when the gleaming knives were slashing around him. In an instant his head was cut off; the old woman was also beheaded, and both bodies were left exposed upon the grass, which was found saturated with blood when a relief party of the Sek-hoan ran forward. On hearing the report of the gun, the villagers at once knew that the savages were out, but before they could reach the spot this dreadful tragedy had already taken place. The burial of the two headless bodies on Sabbath afternoon of the 28th ult. was a very affecting occasion. A large party of armed brethren had to accompany the funeral cortège. The loss of Bun-liong is deeply mourned by the whole church. He was a tall, splendid-looking man, very quiet and unassuming, and one whose whole life was, I believe, under the influence of Divine grace. He seemed to have a long life of usefulness before him, but it has not been ended by this transference to the membership of the Church on high. I feel sad to think of his helpless family, for whom some little provision will no doubt be made.

It may be added here that, while at Lai-sia, the brethren supplied me with further particulars regarding the similarly tragic end of Brother Dzoe. He had gone a short way inland from his station at Sin-kang, and was set upon by a party of mountaineers, who did not cease their attack till his poor, lifeless body lay stretched upon the ground. He, too, is one whose name ought not to be passed by. Brought to a saving knowledge of Christ through the preaching of Mr. Ritchie, he was afterwards trained for the work of the Gospel at Takow, and engaged in successful work there at the time of my arrival in Formosa. He was summoned to a wider field of usefulness when the call reached him to go and become pioneer preacher and evangelist of the Canadian Mission at Tamsui. Of his career there, at a time when he stood alone in active Christian service, I cannot enlarge now, but the day will declare that his humble, self-denying labours were owned and blessed by the Master Himself.

I had great difficulty in getting out from Lai-sia on this occasion. After ten days of continuous rain, the river at the mouth of the valley was much swollen, and a party of the brethren and myself were repeatedly baffled in our attempts to get over. At last, about a dozen strong fellows volunteered to make another extra effort, and we succeeded in reaching the opposite side. While surrounded by them in mid-channel, I found it impossible to stand against the deep, powerful torrent, and was almost miraculously snatched from a watery grave. As there was no possibility of bringing across either of my travelling baskets, I marched along for about ten miles with an old waterproof over my bare body, and had to borrow a Chinese outfit on reaching our friends in the village of Toa-sia.

The native preacher at this Toa-sia station is Brother Kia, who was baptized in Taiwanfoo about two years ago, and who

More about the Sek-hoan. 341

received some training in the city before being sent out at the beginning of the present year. As yet, everything we have seen about Kia has given us unmingled satisfaction. He has fair average ability, and a nice courteous manner, while there appears to be a thoroughness and honesty about his style of working which makes us feel exceedingly thankful. He had not a very favourable report to give me of the state of things in Toa-Sia at this time. There was one woman whom he could recommend for baptism, and she was the only person who received admission on the forenoon of the following Sabbath. He said, too, that he had much difficulty in knowing how to act towards a number of people who attended the services, and were very desirous to receive admission to the Church, but whose knowledge of Chinese is so very limited, as to render it almost impossible that they can attain to an acquaintance with Scripture truth. The difficulty was one I could sympathise with, and one which has often met me in my own work, both at this station and in Po-sia. Of course, all I could do was to advise him to make a point of seeing those people in their homes, of speaking to them in the simplest language, and of praying with and for them, in the hope that they might be led to trust in Christ alone for salvation. Kia is doing better among the children than any of our previous assistants stationed here; twelve of them can write the Romanised Colloquial with great ease, and six boys are daily engaged in reading the Chinese character Scriptures.

We regret that the brethren at Toa-sia should be so much involved in their worldly affairs. Nearly all of them are in debt,

More about the Sek-hoan. 343

and quite a number have little 'cases' on hand, which distract their minds, and lead them to hope more for temporal advantages than for spiritual blessing from their connection with the Church. No doubt, while still almost at the beginning of such a work, one need not be surprised to meet with even much of this. The presence of elements like these ought only to increase our desire to act towards members and adherents in the spirit of patient watchfulness, well assured that our work has a bearing upon the future as well as on the immediate present, and that it is ours to labour on in faith, although the results may greatly fail to come up to the measure of our expectation.

On the return journey, I came directly south from Toa-sia, *via* Chiang-hoa and Ka-gi, to Taiwanfoo. More than usually good opportunities were given us of speaking a word by the way. The people everywhere were extremely civil; particularly so a large crowd which met in an old temple at Po-tau-a, and which it was my privilege to address on a number of important subjects during the half-hour we rested there. As a matter to be looked for at this time of the year, we were greatly delayed in crossing the streams during the four days we were on the way.

7. *Confirming the Churches.*

TAIWANFOO, 26 *November* 1874.—I shall here note down a few encouraging things I met with during my recent visit to some of the Ka-gi villages. Our congregations in that county seem to be making advance in the Divine life, and individuals I met with here and there in the course of my fortnight's sojourn were

Confirming the Churches. 345

evidently speaking and acting under 'the powers of the world to come.' Several of the native brethren accompanied me, and we set out to spend the first Sabbath at Hoan-a-chhan, an aboriginal village about sixteen miles north-east from Taiwanfoo, in which Christian work has been carried on for the past two years. It lies in a rather sparsely populated part of Ka-gi, but one passes through a few towns in going to it, where good opportunities for wayside preaching can always be had.

We reached Hoan-a-chhan on Saturday afternoon to have a pleasant meeting with the brethren that same evening, and on the following day I conducted all the services, our native assistant having gone to preach to a little colony of worshippers which has sprung up in the village of Thau-sia, fully three miles from Hoan-a-chhan, in the direction of Poah-be. At present, the regular hearers in Hoan-a-chhan number about thirty. They are a very poor people, more dull, perhaps, than their fellow-Christians at some of the other stations; and a good deal looked down upon by their crafty and more prosperous Chinese neighbours. Thus, however, it is, that God sometimes passes by the self-sufficient, to make the poor of this world rich in faith, and heirs of the kingdom which He hath promised to them that love Him.

A considerable part of my time on the Sabbath was occupied in examining six persons who wished to receive baptism. After much careful inquiry, I thought that two of these might be admitted. On account of some little irregularity in their family relations, young Tsai and his wife were advised not to come forward at this time. It was with some difficulty I could bring myself to offer this advice. They have both manifested a very teachable and obedient spirit, and will soon be able to read the New Testament in Roman letters. They blundered a good deal in answering, but the agitation of the moment was sufficient to account for this. I love to think of them as being subjects of the Spirit's gracious teaching, and would firmly hope that, in due time, they may come forward to bear good testimony to the truth as it is in Jesus.

Haw-eng was one of the two passed for baptism, and is a married man of about thirty years of age. He reads well, and has done much to keep together and increase the little band of worshippers in this place. Our assistants have spoken of his humble, loving spirit and consistent life, and Dr. Dickson and myself had agreed that he ought to be received.

Teng-ho is the other brother we rejoiced over that quiet Sabbath afternoon. Ok-kau, or Wicked Dog, is the name by which he was formerly known, and it conveyed a true description of his character. He can refer to no particular day when the great change passed upon him. Curiosity brought him to attend the services, and the kindly treatment and unselfishness of the brethren arrested his attention. They did not shun him as one who had become hopelessly poor, and sinful, and miserable. The Gospel,—the like of which he had never listened to before,—he could not understand at first. He was always confusing things, and, like many others placed much more favourably, would often return from worship with a heart entirely unresponsive to the truth. But he held on, thinking that, at the very least, it was pleasant to be hearing about One who was able and willing to help weak sinners like himself. He even commenced to pray in secret, although here his difficulties seemed to increase. How could one pray if there were no tangible object to whom the prayer would be addressed? Teng-ho thinks that about this time, when he commenced to confess sin, and ask God for Jesus' sake to make him a better and a happier man, the Spirit helped him to forsake many evil practices, and truly to desire that he might become an earnest follower of Jesus Christ. He says that he has still many spiritual enemies to contend against, and that he tries daily to lean upon Him who has promised to save to the uttermost.

Surely all this is the doing of the Lord, and may well give rise to feelings of gratitude and holy joy. Oh that God would bestow much of His

Spirit on the feeble instrumentality made use of for the accomplishment of His work! I feel more and more the need of a holy, wise, and loving, Christ-like life amongst our poor people. Much of what we say fails to interest them, but this they can understand.

From Hoan-a-chhan we crossed to Thau-sia, and met with an agreeable surprise on finding that no fewer than ten families here were now meeting statedly for Christian worship. The village is easily reached from our station at Poah-be. It is surrounded by lofty trees, the grateful shade of which is such a luxury in Formosa. Our first sight of it, from the summit of a low range of hills which shuts in the view from the north and west, reminded me of the quiet and comfortable little hamlets of Po-sia, far away from the din and bustle of the outer world, and just such a spot as one would wish for training any people into the fear and service of our God. The present movement commenced through the influence of Eng-sun, a small farmer and rather well-to-do man, who has attended the services at Hoan-a-chhan almost from the time that place was added to our list of stations. His house stands about half a mile from the village, but a lovely little spot of ground there belongs to him, which he has promised to hand over, when the converts are able to build a chapel. On the evening of this visit, about fifty persons came together, and listened with much attention to a long, homely address on the parable of the Prodigal Son. I arranged that the native preacher should meanwhile remain with them. They might have continued their attendance at Hoan-a-chhan ; but unfriendly neighbours kept pilfering from the brethren's houses when the inmates were all away; while even stated work at Thau-sia would add almost nothing to our walking, but rather provide a welcome resting-place between Poah-be and Peh-tsui-khe, Hoan-a-chhan coming in conveniently on the way south again, from this latter place to the city.

Our party started from Thau-sia on Tuesday morning, and reached Peh-tsui-khe the same evening. The road lies through four market-towns, in two of which we had good open-air meetings. Our longest halt was made at Tiam-a-khau, where we saw the residence of Gaw-chi-ko, a wealthy half mandarin half robber-chief, who has attained his present position through personal force of character, and the commission of numberless acts of spoliation among the people of this region. He is said to have about two hundred

Confirming the Churches. 353

armed retainers continually about him. The authorities appear to wink at his on-goings, because of occasional money presents which he sends down to Taiwan-foo, and of the inadequate resources they have for calling so powerful an offender to account.

I spent four days at Peh-tsui-khe, and was much pleased to receive a good report of the congregation. Six months ago, it was with difficulty we could muster an audience of thirty here, but now the regular Sabbath attendances range from eighty to over a hundred. At that time, too, the *Thong-su* or Pi-po-hoan civil officer, with his followers, seemed to spend the greater part of their time in devising schemes for the annoyance and oppression of our poor brethren; whereas they are at present friendly, having destroyed their idols, become punctual in their attendance on Divine worship, and given every reasonable evidence of being sincere and steadfast in their professions of repentance.

The greater number of those who have joined us recently come from a small village named Giam-Cheng, beautifully situated among a low-lying range of hills near Pillow Mountain. In all, there may be about twenty households in that company, one man and his son having attended the services almost from the time of our first visit to Peh-tsui-khe. For two years, no others could be induced to come, fear of the Thong-su prevailing over other considerations in keeping them back. This proved a very severe testing-time for Brother Li and his son, who now no longer require to take turn in going solitarily to worship, and have their minds disturbed about what fresh trouble may be awaiting their return. From the Giamcheng neighbourhood alone there has been an accession of between forty and fifty persons to our congregation. Probably with the exception of Po-sia, I do not know a better place for carrying on hopeful work among the young. A wellconducted school might be rescuing scores of children who came about the chapel, and this ought certainly to be kept in view, even although an extra native assistant may be required.

One serious drawback to the whole work is the want of a proper chapel and schoolroom, with dwelling-house accommodation for the young men in charge. In this direction, however, a great improvement will soon take place. The Mission has secured a most eligible site within the village, and I feel sure the brethren will not fail in doing their part.

Many of them know little of the truth as yet, while others may be actuated by unworthy motives in identifying themselves with us, but after every deduction has been made, I believe we have a band of faithful ones who will form the nucleus of a large and prosperous church.

While visiting about among the people, I called at the house of the Thong-su, who received me with much kindness. The first object which attracted my notice on entering was a large sheet containing the Ten Commandments written in Chinese. It was pasted up on the place usually reserved for idolatrous papers, and revealed at a glance the change which has taken place in the outward conduct of the man. We had a long friendly conversation, during the course of which I could see that his interest seemed truly awakened in regard to spiritual things. Here, also, my

Confirming the Churches. 357

heart was gladdened to meet with a poor erring brother from Poah-be, whose long absence from worship and fall into scandalous sin, laid upon us the sorrowful duty of suspending him from Church privileges. I was not previously aware that Lian-chhun was a son-in-law of the Peh-tsui-khe Thong-su, through whom he came under very bad influence after his baptism, and was led to forsake the company of God's people at Poah-be. Since his father-in-law commenced to show a forgiving spirit towards our Peh-tsui-khe brethren, Lian-chhun has been regular in his attendance on Sabbath, and has repeatedly expressed himself to the preacher as feeling most unhappy on account of his weakness in the hour of temptation. He expressed himself in a very penitent way that day I saw him, and seemed overjoyed at the probability of being once more numbered among those who are welcomed to the table of the Lord.

Another interesting circumstance connected with my visit to Giam-cheng at this time was the open destruction of the idols, ancestral tablets, and idolatrous pictures, belonging to a number of people who had resolved to cast in their lot with the disciples of Jesus. Some of the tablets had been preserved for over a hundred years, and were covered with names of deceased relations, whose continued presence those pieces of wood are intended to represent. A copy was taken of all the names and dates upon them, as likely to prove useful in deciding certain questions which might arise about the rightful possession of fields; and then, with the wooden idols—some of which were very old and greatly disfigured—they were brought out, and placed beside the other objects in a wide, open space before the house. There were about thirty brethren present, who gathered round and joined in singing one of our well-known hymns. When prayer had been offered, a light was applied to the heap in front of us, which was speedily reduced to ashes. I afterwards spoke to those good-natured, simple people of the only way of salvation through the blood of Christ, exhorting those of them who had renounced idolatry to a living faith in Him, and declaring to all, that, without holiness, no man could see the Lord.

On returning to the chapel, I had the native preacher to assist me in examining candidates for baptism. Only one man had been previously admitted at this station, and his brother was the first who now came forward. Anything I already knew of Iau-li was of a favourable character; and, as he reads well and answered nearly all my questions, I felt that his request could not be denied, and that we ought to welcome him into our midst.

Brother Chheng-sui was another who was examined and passed for baptism. He, also, is a good reader; and, in the case of young persons who have had ample opportunity for learning the easily-acquired Romanised form of the language, we have come to regard this accomplishment very much in the light of one important qualification for admission to Church ordinances. Now that the New Testament in so simple a form has been prepared for their especial benefit, we feel that there is a necessity to insist on the duty and the privilege of their being able to consult it for themselves. Chheng-sui is only eighteen years of age, and the principal support of his widowed mother. One cannot but like his frank, amiable manner.

He is said to have been always a well-behaved boy, very unselfish, and one who loved his mother by doing everything he could to make her happy. His knowledge of Scripture is tolerably good, and I cannot refuse to believe that, in some measure at least, the Spirit has taken of the things of Christ and shown them unto him.

Brother Li and his son Hut from Gi-am-cheng, with another man named Tsu-Ong, were also received for baptism on this occasion. These five candidates had all been hearers since our services commenced at Peh-tsui-khe. They manifested a very proper spirit during a recent time of persecution there, and did much by their example to strengthen and comfort the other brethren. Hut is a particularly promising boy, a fluent reader, sharp, and yet modest; and one who, in a year or two, may do good work as a teacher. The two others cannot read, but there is reason to hope that they have been brought to feel their helplessness as poor sinners in the sight of God, and to trust in Christ alone for salvation.

The above-named brethren received baptism at Hoan-a-chhan. A goodly company of friends from Thau-sia and Peh-tsui-khe were present at the services. It was a pleasant, busy time for the worshippers at Hoan-a-chhan, and I was glad to see that they treated their fellow-converts with so much kindness and hospitality. It is very interesting for one to notice the influence of Christianity in improving the manners, social customs, and outward appearance of a people like this. The loud coarseness, the bad language, the filth, and even the rags, give way to gentleness, courtesy, cleanliness, and comfort. What a wonderful reformer was Christ!

I set out for the city on Monday morning. The journey was a lightsome and pleasant one. Amid innumerable shortcomings on our part, a few more had been brought to taste and see that the Lord is gracious. I felt strong and refreshed, and more than ever assured that the name of Jesus would be glorified among the hill-people of Formosa.

8. *The Japanese Trouble.*

TAIWANFOO, 16 *December* 1874.— Fully two years ago, an open boat was cast upon the southern coast of Formosa, and its Japanese subjects from Loochoo cruelly murdered by a party of Baw-tan savages. On a claim for compensation being presented to the Chinese Government, the reply was made that those tribes on the eastern side of the island were not subjects of the Empire; whereupon Japan took the matter into her own hands. A large military expedition was landed at Long-kiau, and very soon that part of the country became a base of operations for proceeding further inland. Of course, this action caused any amount of dissatisfaction at Peking. Strong remonstrances were made against what was called 'invading the territory of a friendly Power.' Control over the whole island was now insisted upon, and it was claimed that China alone had the right of dealing with those native tribes. To all this, however, the Japanese gave very little heed. Military law was proclaimed over the greater part of the South Cape, the position of the newcomers became more and more strengthened, and there was not the slightest appearance of withdrawal, even after the savages had been severely punished.

The Japanese Trouble. 365

As diplomatic resources had failed to bring about a settlement, the Chinese at length bestirred themselves to prepare for the worst. An Imperial Commissioner named Sim Po Seng came and took charge of the operations in Formosa, in which duty he was ably seconded by M. Giquel of the Foochow Arsenal. Their action clearly assumed that the Japanese might advance northward, mud forts being erected at a great many points along the western seaboard, and the garrisons increased at every important centre from Tamsui to Pi-thau. Great pains were taken to put Taiwanfoo into as good a condition of defence as the circumstances would permit. An extensive fort was erected a little to the north-west of it, gangs of workmen were kept busily engaged in repairing the walls, soldiers were to be met with at every important point, and the strongly-guarded city gates were all but closed for a time.

It will be obvious that these preparations could not fail to have rather an unsettling influence on the quiet progress of our work. I had good opportunity for seeing this while travelling from Tamsui to Taiwanfoo about three months ago. During the nine days I was on the way, one could hear no end of remark about the Japanese, and at several of our stations, there had been a large increase to the audiences on Sabbath by persons who thought that admission to the Church might afford some kind of protection in view of the coming struggle.

Ka-gi city is the place which has come more prominently before our notice in connection with this war scare. The region after which this city takes its name occupies the middle-western part of the

The Japanese Trouble. 367

island, and forms the largest and most populous of the Formosan counties. We require to travel right through it while visiting our Sek-hoan stations, and although there is encouraging work going on among the Pi-po-hoan in Ka-gi, our great desire is to begin stated preaching in some purely Chinese community there. No spot seems so inviting as the county city itself. It is central, and contains many thousands who have never heard the Gospel, while Christian work carried on at that centre, in the very presence of the higher officials, as it were, would greatly help in overcoming the opposition we meet with in other parts of the county.

Indeed, so much did we feel the necessity for pushing in this direction, that, months before the landing of the Japanese expedition, one of our assistants was sent to Ka-gi with instructions to take up his residence in a roadside inn of the place, engage in daily preaching, and see what opportunities there might be for purchasing or renting premises in which to begin regular work. Brother Pa did good service at that time, and met with no serious difficulty in having open-air meetings, and in selling a large stock of Gospels, pamphlets, and tracts. Soon, however, the people were alarmed about rumours of war, and Church members came to be accused of going about collecting information that might enable a hostile force to come and destroy Chinese rule in the island, and bring it once more into the possession of foreigners. This closed the first of our attempts to effect an entrance into the city of Ka-gi.

Our next effort promises to be more successful, and has taken place at a much earlier date than we could have anticipated.

The Japanese Trouble. 369

It is still but a few weeks since an immeasurable feeling of relief was experienced in Formosa on news arriving that war was averted, and that so great a blessing had been brought about very largely, if not altogether, through the services of our British Minister at Peking, Mr. Wade. We obtained some of the good results of this almost at once. Influential Chinamen became markedly respectful, and all sorts of questions were asked about the nation whose representative could wield such power. Our preachers, too, were in great demand, and found it impossible to supply all the information that was asked for. No one seems to have any difficulty in understanding the position, and many millions of crackers would certainly be let off were Mr. Wade himself to put in an appearance. I tried to give the thing a somewhat practical turn by sending two

2 A

of our young men to see what more could be done in the way of obtaining a foothold in Ka-gi. They have been absent for about ten days, and their first report now lies before me. It is very cheering. The people everywhere are most friendly, and every facility is being given for the prosecution of their work. I have arranged to meet them at the south gate on Tuesday first, when, in all probability, arrangements will be made for taking up our permanent abode among the spiritually destitute thousands of this heathen city. We feel the step to be an important one in the progress of our work in Formosa, and our constant prayer is that we may be guided aright, and that a double portion of the Spirit may rest on the native preacher who may be stationed here.

9. A Narrow Escape.

TAIWANFOO, 7 *February* 1875.—Missionary work at Peh-tsui-khe has just received a check, and in order to give an intelligible account of the matter, it will be necessary to begin by saying something about the market-town of Tiam-a-khau, which lies about five miles west of the hamlet where our chapel is situated.

A great many of the people in Tiam-a-khau belong to the Chinese clan or family of the surname Gaw, and the local head of this clan is Gaw-chi-ko, a notorious character, whose lawless deeds have been a source of annoyance and anxiety to the authorities for years past. Through a long course of trickery and oppression, he is said now to be possessed of immense wealth. His large residence is just outside of Tiam-a-khau, all the houses connected with it being built within strong bamboo stockades, around which many armed retainers are always kept in readiness to defend the place against mandarin or popular attack.

When our work began among the Pi-po-hoan at Peh-tsui-khe, Gaw-chi-ko was told about it, and was quiet for a time, but soon came to see that the movement was one which could give no countenance to his schemes of selfishness and cruelty. For one thing, he quite objected to influential foreigners from Taiwanfoo paying periodical visits to any of the villages on the east side of Tiam-a-khau. Under a fear that strong measures might one day be taken against him by the Chinese authorities, he had ever been opposed to anything that might cut off his way of retreat into the inaccessible mountain region beyond. As for the newly-established foreign

A Narrow Escape. 373

Church in that direction, it was enough for him that it was influencing the people for good, and was a thing which could not come within range of his own sympathy or control.

Before the commencement of our work at Peh-tsui-khe, it was no uncommon occurrence for Gaw-chi-ko to order out twenty or thirty of the Pi-po-hoan to work for him, giving them in return a starvation allowance of rice, with hard words and blows should any of them show unwillingness to comply with his demands. His present policy is to increase their burden tenfold, and do everything he can to keep matters *in statu quo*. And yet, since those aborigines have come under educational and Christian influences, I can confidently say that it would be difficult to find anywhere a more quiet, inoffensive, and law-abiding people. Petty hieving with them is wholly a thing of the past. They don't gamble now, and one will listen in vain to hear bad language from the lips of any of our converts. Even their heathen neighbours acknowledge that, both in character and condition, they have undergone a very decided change for the better, and we ourselves regarded Peh-tsui-khe as one of the most prosperous and hopeful of our fourteen stations. During the past two months, the brethren had been busy in preparing materials for the erection of a new chapel, and it was while making arrangements with them for the completion of this work that a long course of petty persecution ended in the more serious trouble about to be referred to.

I left Taiwanfoo on 15th January, and spent the remainder of that week at Peh-tsui-khe. Everything was then quiet, excepting the usual rumours of an attack by the Tiam-a-khau people, and of an objec-

A Narrow Escape. 375

tion which Gaw-chi-ko had mentioned to some of our brethren against the erection of the proposed new chapel. He said that, as it would interfere with the *Fung-shui*— or imagined spiritual influences—of a grave belonging to him, it would be better for every one concerned not to persist in building on the present site. This fresh objection appeared to be a very unreasonable one because (1) Gaw-chi-ko's men had been repeatedly told that the new chapel would be only a few feet larger than, and built upon exactly the same site as, the old one ; (2) the old chapel was situated at a distance of nearly four hundred paces from the grave in question, and during the twelve months it had been used as a place for Christian worship, no objection of this kind had ever been heard of. In fact, the heathen people of the neighbourhood said that this Fung-shui affair was a mere pretence.

I instructed our brethren to go on with the work, and, meanwhile, went to take possession of mission premises we had acquired in the city of Ka-gi, returning to Peh-tsui-khe on the 22d. During my absence, a number of loose, idle characters from Tiam-a-khau had been visiting the place, and on the following Monday two messengers arrived from Gaw-chi-ko to say that he wished to see me about the Fung-shui business. Now, it so happened that I was busy at the time, and had, moreover, no particular desire to undertake a five miles' walk on the invitation of one who had been acting in such a high-handed and oppressive way. Accordingly, after a little friendly talk and some explanation, the messengers were told that either Dr. Dickson or myself could always be found in Tai-wanfoo, and that Gaw-chi-ko might call

A Narrow Escape. 377

there, or even write to us, and we should be very willing to consider his statement.

I left Peh-tsui-khe on the 27th, and on the following day arrived in our chapel at Thau-sia, a village some twenty miles to the south. In about an hour after, two of the Peh-tsui-khe Christians abruptly entered, and said that an armed band had attacked several of the brethren's houses on the previous night, that one woman was lying dangerously ill from spear-wounds, six bullocks had been stolen, outhouses burned down, and several of the families left destitute of money, clothes, and cooking utensils. They added that, although the robbers' faces were disguised, all the people who had been attacked were certain that they came from Tiam-a-khau, while the woman who was so severely wounded distinctly recognised one of her assailants as being a desperate fellow in the service of Gaw-chi-ko.

Early the following morning, I hurried off for Peh-tsui-khe and arrived there about sunset; not, however, before meeting with several of Gaw-chi-ko's men who were journeying towards Tiam-a-khau. I found that the statement of the two brethren was correct in every particular. The poor woman already referred to appeared to be on the point of death. In her attempt to escape, she had climbed about six feet up a small tree at the back of the house, and while in that position, had received some very severe wounds. I saw the side of this tree, and the ground below still covered with blood. One man had been speared in the ankle, another suffered from a deep cut in the arm, and nearly all the bed and body clothing of the two families I called on that evening

A Narrow Escape. 379

had been carried off. As it was now quite dark, I endeavoured to calm their minds, and said that, on the morrow, I hoped to call at all their houses for particulars, with the view of trying to help them. There were some sad, anxious hearts at our prayer-meeting afterwards.

Feeling somewhat tired, I did not sit very late that night. The room I occupied was one of three, in a line, and all under the same roof, the entire structure being of bamboo framework, grass roof, and slim wattle-and-dab walls. The native preacher and his wife had possession of the one little end room, and myself of the other, the middle apartment doing service as a dining-room and place for receiving visitors. The building was a mere dilapidated hut, and stood about twenty feet from the temporary chapel, which was made of the same materials and in similar style. There were few other houses in the neighbourhood, as the people live very much scattered over this quiet and hilly part of the country.

It would be about midnight when I was startled on hearing people rushing through the fence which surrounds our chapel ground, and by the bright glare of many lights moving rapidly round the house. I jumped up to find that my bedroom was already on fire, and on looking out through the bamboo bars which served as a window, I could see a crowd of ferocious-looking ruffians setting fire to the chapel, and to the roof of our own house. One could take in the position at a glance. It was Gaw-chi-ko's men out on one of their terrible raids. They seemed like demons as, with blackened faces and long knives in their hands, they darted about under the bright glare of the burning chapel. I called out

A Narrow Escape. 381

for assistance, but learned afterwards that the preacher and his wife, with some brethren who were sleeping in an adjoining hut, had made their escape.

Supposing they would hardly dare to attack a foreigner, I attempted to get out by the door of the mid-room, but was immediately driven back by the spears which were levelled at me, and which for a moment I warded off with the Chinese blanket held over my arm. I shouted out that the British Consul would have them punished if they persisted, but their knives and spears were again brandished in front of me, and struck frequently into the little blanket. On retreating into the preacher's room, I was at once pursued by ten or a dozen of these cowards, who were evidently afraid to follow one singly into the smaller apartment. They kept poking their spears in at the door, and then commenced to break down the thin partition on my left. While standing here at the foot of the small bed one of the spears was thrust through the lathing and passed within an inch of my body.

The place now began to fill with smoke, the dry grass roofing being on fire all round, and the chapel itself enveloped in flames. My own little bedroom was crumbling to ashes, and continually the heated air in the blazing bamboos would become expanded and burst like the report of so many pistols. At this moment those in the mid-room retreated to the outside, when I tried hard again to follow them away from the burning house, the heat and smoke of which had now become almost insupportable. The sight which met my eyes at the door was certainly alarming. There was nothing but fire and smoke all over the chapel, and there

A Narrow Escape. 383

seemed something almost fiendish in the determination of that crowd as they stood back awaiting my exit with uplifted knives and spears. I once more rushed inside, and badly injured my hands and bare feet in trying to break a way of escape out from the back, and while thus engaged, some one smashed the bars of the window-opening in front and cast in a burning torch, which began to set the loose straw of the bed on fire.

I quite gave it up at this point, committed myself to God, and for the last time dashed out, expecting nothing but to be cast upon those awful spears. To my surprise, the whole party was seen to be quickly moving away to the right. The wind had somewhat risen, and they could no longer endure the smoke from the burning chapel behind, nor the flames which were beginning to lick over the house before which they had been standing. Having no other clothing about me save my sleeping-shirt, I sprang out from the door, climbed over an earth embankment on the left, then got severely scratched in tearing through a thick prickly fence higher up, and ended by tumbling down into a ditch, where I lay for a minute or two half unconscious, and trembling on account of the intense coldness of the night.

On lifting my head above the tall grass here, I could see several torches spread over fields on the other side, as if search were being made for those who had just escaped. Without raising myself, therefore, I crept slowly along, got up into a hillside somewhat further off; and lay concealed there till a retreat was sounded, and the whole gang ran off in the direction of Tiam-a-khau. It was still some hours before daybreak when the preacher found me and supplied me with a pair of old Chinese trousers. We soon after started through the mountain paths, and ran a good part of the way north to the city of Ka-gi. On entering the South Gate, there was great excitement to see a foreigner travelling without a hat, and having his bare legs streaked with blood. Some of them recognised me as being the one who had been there frequently of late trying to obtain premises that might serve as a chapel.

We at once proceeded to the *Yamen* of the District Magistrate, where not only the large court, but the walls, and even the roofs of the adjoining houses, became speedily covered with a curious and excited crowd. There was an almost endless amount of discussion as to what might be the cause of the disturbance, and the Magistrate would keep insisting that the Christians must be to blame. At last I got thoroughly nettled, and said that he ought to know that this was not the time to go into the merits of the case, that he could plainly see the condition I was in, half-naked and having nothing to eat. I said I was quite within my right in claiming his protection, and that I would now leave and have the whole case reported to his superiors down south. This little incident produced an immediate result; for, soon after, I was asked into a side-room, where a small tubful of rice and fourteen boiled eggs were placed before me. A new Chinese quilt was also procured, a sedan chair placed at my disposal, and I was sent away the two-days' journey to Taiwanfoo, under an escort of armed soldiers.

Three of the brethren from Peh-tsui-

A Narrow Escape. 387

khe reached the capital before me, to inform the Doctor of what had taken place, but—with Mrs. Dickson—he happened to be in Poah-be at the time of their arrival. I came in a few hours after them on Sabbath afternoon, and went on the following morning to confer with Mr. Ritchie as to what might be our best course in the circumstances. The Consul has already called the attention of the higher officials to the matter, and we hope that something may be done to bring order out of all this confusion. A recent messenger from Peh-tsui-khe informs us that the County Magistrate at Ka-gi, accompanied by about two hundred soldiers, visited the scene of the outrage last Monday, and returned again without going in the direction of Tiam-a-khau. This messenger also states that Gaw-chi-ko has sent men to beat gongs throughout the region and summon his followers, who are now assembled in great force. Meanwhile, our hearts are pained to think of our defenceless and sorely-tried brethren. They are afraid to stay in their homes, and spend much of their time in hiding-places among the mountains. I have suffered myself a good deal from severe scratches and the night exposure. My watch, clothes, and nearly everything I had with me at the time, have been destroyed, the object of our poor miserable enemies plainly being, not robbery, but murder.

10. *Another North Journey*.

TAIWANFOO, 25 *April* 1875.—The American Consul at Amoy accompanied me on my recent visit to our northern stations, and we started from Taiwanfoo on 10th *ult*. The first night was spent at Hoan-a-chhan, where we had a refreshing little prayer-meeting with the native brethren immediately after supper. It was pleasant to notice the acts of kindness shown to them by my travelling companion.

Surely our fellow-countrymen in China are not aware of the extent they might assist the progress of our work. It is, indeed, a red-letter day when some European merchant or Consul undertakes a long journey, and really tries to give us a lift. Thank God, we do meet with those who are both able and willing to help, and thank God for the noble Christian officers who sometimes visit us. Men like Captain Bax of H.M.S. *Dwarf* will have an honoured place in the hagiology of the Church in Formosa.

Hau-hi is the preacher now stationed at Hoan-a-chhan. He was born of Chinese parents on the mainland, and was brought to Formosa by a party of Sek-hoan, who were over assisting in the suppression of the Tai-ping Rebellion. He has an intimate knowledge of the aboriginal language, and this might be turned to good account, even among some of the savage tribes. He had a favourable report to give me of the work at Hoan-a-chhan.

We put up for the second night at Gi-am-cheng, a little village about twenty minutes' walk from the place where our Peh-tsui-khe chapel stood. As we passed through Tiam-a-khau on the way to it, my presence there caused no little commotion. I suppose it was thought that our visit had some reference to the late outrage, and that a number of the ill-favoured persons around us would now be brought to justice.

Giam-cheng will henceforth be the

centre of our work in this region. The largest group of worshippers is to be found here, and a chapel among them would, in some respects, be even more convenient than one at Peh-tsui-khe. The brethren assembled from all quarters on the night of our visit. Poor people! they are certainly having much to try them at present, and one cannot feel too thankful for the patient and forgiving spirit they have shown. Our preacher has not yet returned to his post here, nor have they had any place in which to meet for worship since the chapel was burned down. Indeed, so constant were the hostile rumours after the second attack that, for weeks, many of the converts absented themselves from their houses, and kept under concealment in the woods and glens further east of this. We had another pleasant meeting on the morning of our departure from Giam-cheng. It was held among the ashes of the chapel-buildings at Peh-tsui-khe, and—like Bethel of old—the spot was then made sacred to us.

We arrived in the city of Ka-gi on 13th *ult.*, and a few hours after, I received an official communication about the late disturbances at Peh-tsui-khe. It stated that four men of the Gaw clan were now in prison, that the native converts had received an indemnity of one hundred dollars, and that two notifications had been issued, in which favourable reference was made to the Christian religion, and all classes warned against molesting people who embraced it. Now, there was hardly anything about this decision we could approve of. The four men of the Gaw clan happened to be certain poor, hired wretches, who were at that moment having a glorious time of dissipation in one

Another North Journey. 393

of the outhouses of the Magistrate's *Ya-men*, the property which had been stolen amounted in value to over three hundred dollars, while the larger of the two notifications made a number of most glaring misstatements regarding the simple facts of the case. Having the clearest evidence that Gaw-chi-ko himself is the real offender, we surely must object when it is stated that this notoriously law-defying chief of Tiam-a-khau has brought our assailants to justice, and will continue to exert himself for the preservation of peace. The mandarins well know who ought to be reckoned with, not only for those outrages at Peh-tsui-khe, but for very many previous acts of robbery and oppression, and I have little doubt they would now take the opportunity of making a clearance in this part of the country, were it not that the Emperor's death, two months ago, has thrown many things into a state of uncertainty and confusion. It would require a strong military force to attempt the arrest of Gaw-chi-ko and his formidable band of ruffians, and one feels inclined to believe the current rumours that, fearing the consequences of being concerned in the attack on a British subject, he has paid in a very heavy bribe to the authorities for having matters hushed up as quietly and as quickly as possible.

Meanwhile, I rejoice to think that all these things are falling out for the furtherance of the Gospel, and nowhere more evidently than in Ka-gi itself. It is the Lord's doing, and to His holy name be all the praise. Only a few months ago, we were beginning almost to despair of securing premises of any kind in the county city. On the occasion of a visit there in December last, men were sent through all the main streets to beat a huge gong and warn people that, whoever sold or rented a house to the foreigner would be buried alive ; none of the innkeepers would receive our party on the next visit ; I purchased the present house on 21st January ; and now, we could have our choice of a site for building, or of premises sufficiently large to accommodate the crowds who are willing to give us a respectful hearing. Not that the common people ever did much to thwart us. Many of these had received benefit at our Mission Hospital, but did not dare to act in a friendly way, because of opposition from persons belonging to the official and literary classes.

The authorities at present are only too glad to say anything that will conciliate, and it is certainly somewhat significant to come across a statement like this in a proclamation which was recently issued by the Officer administering the affairs of Ka-gi :— 'Wherefore I, the Magistrate, enjoin and expect all manner of people, in all the County, to know and understand that the British missionaries' teaching is none other than the exhorting of men to be good ; that their renting of land and building of chapels is in accordance with an established Treaty ; and that they must be allowed to do these things as they themselves think fit.' Of course, one has to avoid the mistake of attaching too much value to any such testimony. Chinese officials are a slippery race; and, after all, their undoubted opposition to the missionary is not much to be wondered at.

I think Dr. Dickson's medical work in Ka-gi will be most helpful at this time. When blind persons receive their sight, and poor sufferers are sent away cured and comfortable, we need only to be at hand for gathering in the abundant good results.

I am firmly persuaded we are on the threshold of a grand work here. One would like to have wings, or the power of being in several places at the same time. Lord, help! Keep us from making blunders at the commencement, give all needed grace, and speedily bring thousands around us into the light and liberty of the Gospel!

After spending only one night at Ka-gi, we continued our journey next day, and, about dark, reached a village called Kiu-kiong-na, some fifty Chinese *li* to the north-east of the city. As none of the people there would accommodate our party, we slept in a ruinous little temple outside; where, with the dumb idols overlooking us, we experienced the nearness of our Heavenly Father, and felt none the less assured of His goodness in bringing us thus far.

The following day was Sabbath, but we thought it well to make a very short stage, through Lim-ki-po on to Tsu-chip, a good-sized market-town, where I thought there might be favourable opportunities for having some open-air preaching. In this, however, we were disappointed, as the place was filled with rude soldiers from Canton, who were waiting for another larger party, to begin the construction of a road across the mountains. The dialect they spoke was unintelligible to us, and they behaved in rather a quarrelsome way, so that we were compelled to remain indoors. Lim-ki-po and Tsu-chip contain a Chinese population from the Chin-chew region, and in both places the inhabitants have repeatedly treated us with kindness, and listened with marked attention to our

Another North Journey. 399

message. Lim-ki-po is only a day's journey from Ka-gi city, while one day more—beyond it, to the north—brings us to the country of the Tsui-hoan, which is within ten miles of Po-sia.

We arrived at Lake Candidius on the 15th, and spent two days in that neighbourhood. I then took an opportunity of making a careful circuit of the Lake in one of the native canoes, as it was desirable to ascertain what outlet there was for the water, and gain a better knowledge of the stream-system further west. Some of the quiet nooks and coves around the lake are spots of surpassing loveliness; and while our canoe would go shooting across, and the cry of the startled wild-fowl break the silence from time to time, one could not but look up, far up, to the infinitely great Maker and Preserver of all. I regretted there were fewer opportunities for preaching here than upon any previous occasion, the bulk of the people being in a state of almost hopeless intoxication. Probably, in less than a hundred years the Tsui-hoan will be known only by name. The males among them are rapidly being slain by simple downright laziness and drink, and the neighbouring Chinese always succeed in carrying off their best-looking daughters. The more immediate hindrance to bringing them under the influence of the Gospel is our ignorance of their language. Some of them do understand a little Chinese, but the great mass of them not a sentence. Pai-ta-buh, the chief, is said to be over ninety years of age. He is a thorough old sot, although still active, and not without some influence among his people. One cannot but pray that He with whom all things are possible may open a way for the ingathering, not only of this benighted people, but of the Chinese to the west, and even of those large unvisited tribes in the mountain region on the eastern side of the island.

Our party entered Po-sia on the afternoon of the 17th, and at once proceeded to O-gu-lan, where the brethren were delighted to see us, and tried in every way to make us comfortable. It was most encouraging to learn that, during my long absence, the three little congregations had enjoyed another season of peace, and were making steady advancement in the right direction. Here I was sorry to part from my travelling companion, as his duties required him to push on to Tam-sui without further delay. A large party of our brethren escorted him for two days through the belt of savage territory he had to cross before reaching Chiang-hoa. He expressed himself as being much pleased with all he saw at those northern stations, and I feel sure he would be glad to hear of the work spreading from village to village, till the people in Po-sia, and over the whole island, are brought to a saving knowledge of Christ. My only regret was that he could not remain for the large interesting meetings we had at O-gu-lan on the Sabbath.

I arranged that our united Sacramental services should be held at Toa-lam, and in view of this was kept busy for two days at each of the three chapels. It was satisfactory to find that no cases of discipline had to be dealt with, while the careful examination of about fifty candidates resulted in five men and five women being passed for baptism. The afternoon congregation numbered about six hundred, some of the people coming from distant scattered villages, and all of them showing

Another North Journey. 403

an amount of interest which was truly gratifying.

It is well to think of the remarkably fine opportunity we have in Po-sia at present. Our work has brought the place into considerable prominence of late, and I should not be surprised if a large number of Chinese soldiers and emigrants soon found their way into it. Now is the time for us to build up and extend with all our might. I feel much satisfied that the three chapels are nearing completion. They are made of sun-dried bricks, and covered with tiles, instead of the usual grass; each of them having also an upper story or loft for our own personal accommodation. In the Toa-lam building, this upper gallery is quite a comfortable place in which to sleep. It is both wide and cleanly, and is carried round the platform on three sides, leaving the middle part open, and giving the whole interior an appearance like some of the little country churches in Scotland. This chapel could not be put up in Ka-gi or in Taiwanfoo under a thousand dollars, but materials and work are cheaper in Po-sia. It is the first building there on which any mission money from England has been expended. The erection of it had been such a large undertaking, that I promised to send fifty dollars for finishing the roof. We think the brethren are much to be commended in thus showing the value they attach to Christian ordinances. Their example has been very stimulating at the other stations. One of the adherents—a worshipper who has not yet received baptism —gave twenty dollars to the building fund of the Toa-lam chapel and schoolroom.

On the second Wednesday of my visit,

we had the most interesting meeting of the Church children which has yet been held in Po-sia. One hundred and forty children from the three stations met in the chapel at Toa-lam, where an abundant supply of refreshments was served out, and an effort made to tell them of the Sabbath-schools in England. The native preachers also addressed them. Beng-ho spoke in Sek-hoan, thus filling one's heart with eager anticipation to think that God has already given us a way of declaring spiritual truth to hundreds who know little or nothing of Chinese. It is to the music part of the service we feel most attracted in any such gathering of the Po-sia children. The heartiness with which they sing is very inspiring. The Sek-hoan brethren have had no difficulty in adapting several of their own native tunes for the purposes of Christian worship, and some of these have a great amount of simplicity and plaintive sweetness about them; while others lead off with a dash of triumph and hopefulness which would scatter the fears and brighten up the prospects of Faint-heart himself. One of the tunes has been named after dear old Elder Bun, who never saw Po-sia, but who offered many a prayer for the increase and further enlightenment of the brethren there; another is from the Tsui-hoan; a third, the work of one of our deacons; a fourth, contributed by a blind brother at O-gu-lan, and all the others have been adapted from the old native song-tunes into their present Christian use.

We have decided on opening a large central school in Po-sia for the benefit of the children connected with our three congregations. The ordinary village-schools are very unsatisfactory, both in their method of teaching and on account of heathenish practices which the scholars have to go through. We feel that our very utmost must be done for the young people around us. They are the hope of the Church, and any marked improvement among this class tells in two directions, not only influencing the fathers and mothers, but clearing the way for more rapid progress in time to come.

My journey out from Po-sia at this time was an unusually trying one, and attended with no small amount of danger. Early on 7th April, a party of one hundred and three met by appointment at O-gu-lan. Over seventy of these were brethren from different villages, and the others were non-Christian Chinamen and Sek-hoan who came to take advantage of the escort. On the first day's march it was with the utmost difficulty we succeeded in fording two deep rivers, against the strongly-rushing waters of which it would have been impossible to swim had any of us been carried away. We spent that night in a deep ravine among the mountains, where the ground is trod by few save roving bands of savages intent upon head-hunting, or in the pursuit of game. It was pitch dark when we halted, and the rain fell in torrents, while ever and anon heavy stones from the mountain-wall on our right would get loosened and come thundering down. Every man of the party wished himself back again in Po-sia. Of course, sleep was out of the question. One of my native friends considerately placed a deerskin over the stones on which I lay, but the whole pass soon became flooded, and we could only stand there under the pouring rain.

We set out again before daybreak on

Another North Journey. 409

the morning of the 8th, and soon reached a high hill, which required no little exertion to get over. After leaving it, our way lay over the bed of a stream, and through a deep gorge about a couple of miles long, and so narrow at some points, that one's walking-stick placed horizontally could all but touch the lofty walls on either side. I never feel quite comfortable here, it being a place where the savages could easily work terrible havoc. On coming to it, it is our usual practice to plod along in silence, headed by ten or a dozen of the brethren with their guns ready for instant use. On this occasion, it was impossible to enter, as a mass of earth had fallen in and dammed up the water to a depth of twelve or fourteen feet. As there was no help for it, several of the party swam forward and somehow reached the plateau overhead, where, from the mass of rattan lying about, they formed a strong rope, one end of which was fastened to the foot of a tree, and the other flung down to the party waiting below. Holding on by this rope, and with our feet against the sheer wall before us, we all took turn in clambering up, and then continued our journey through jungle, where the way had literally to be cut before us. But I need not pursue the subject. We arrived at Toa-sia about dark on the 9th, weak and thoroughly soaked, our little hardships being very quickly forgotten under the kindly attention of our dear Sek-hoan brethren.

After a brief stay here, several native friends accompanied me to Lai-sia. At certain times of the year even this short journey is one which cannot be attempted. We were fortunate now in finding an old lumbering boat at the Tai-kah River, but

Another North Journey. 411

succeeded in fording the Tai-an, only by holding hands and making a strong dash across. The Church at Lai-sia continues to make progress. There were three admissions at this time, and another brother was elected to fill the place of Elder Bun-liong, who was recently cut off by savages. I regret that the Lai-sia people are still much exposed to danger from this source. Five little towers have been erected on the tops of neighbouring hills, in which armed watchmen are stationed to raise an alarm when the savages are out.

My subsequent stay at Toa-sia was a very pleasant one. We had four admissions, and no cases of discipline. I feel ever so thankful that there does seem to be an increase of spiritual life in this little Church; a conclusion which I do not think I arrived at hastily, but only after seeing much of the brethren at the chapel and in their own homes. They have rented another large schoolroom in the village, and a teacher has been engaged by them at a salary of seventy dollars a year. The importance of this step is apparent, and we shall not only watch the movement with deep interest, but try to help it in every way we can.

I praise and bless the Lord for all that my eyes have seen during those weeks of travel. I met with souls grieved on account of sin, some asking the way heavenward, and others already in possession of that peace which flows from simple, childlike trust in Jesus.

11. *Murder of Un Ong.*

TAIWANFOO, 30 *April* 1877.—Gaw-chi-ko and his men at Tiam-a-khau are still violent in their persecution of our native brethren in the Ka-gi county. The events of January 1875 were dealt with by the authorities in such a feeble way, that they are evidently emboldened to carry out the threat of exterminating Christianity in that part of the island. Their latest attack had a very tragic ending, for the murder of Brother Ong of Ka-poa-soa must now be added to the long list of their misdeeds. My colleague, Mr. Smith—who joined the mission last year—became intimate with this brother shortly before his death, and thought there was something altogether remarkable about his history. While still a youth, Ong's activity and force of character brought him into collision with Gaw-chi-ko, whose henchmen waylaid him one evening, and left him by the roadside with both his eyes gouged out. He soon recovered from this calamity, and although stone blind, continued to be the most active man in the place. After coming under the power of God's grace, he entirely forgave his enemies, and turned all his influence into the service of the Church. He even testified for Christ before Gaw-chi-ko himself, who became so far reconciled that he offered to advance money, and place him in a lucrative business at Tiam-a-khau. The chief probably thought that this would be the readiest way to arrest the progress of our work, but Ong's answer was, 'We followers of Jesus Christ cannot enter into partnership with unbelievers.'

In further explanation of what has just taken place, it is necessary to add that, last summer, one of the Christians at Ka-poa-soa had his cattle stolen by several bad characters, under the leadership of a man called Chiong-hin. Some of our brethren caught this man in the act of carrying off the cattle; but on being appealed to, the local officer refused to do anything in the case, because the injured people were said to have taken the law into their own hands. After his release, the villager Chiong-hin openly declared that he would have his revenge yet, and this, particularly, upon Un Ong, who had been active in trying to secure fair-play for his fellow-Christians.

Such was the position of affairs on 14th *inst.*, on which day Ong had occasion to go and receive some money due to him by a man at Tiam-a-khau. He was accompanied by his son Un Bok, eleven years of age, and by a young man—Hiong Baw-chhun—of the Ka-poa-soa congregation. They had reached a place called Gu-tiau-po-thau on the return journey, when they were set upon by seven or eight armed men led by Chiong-hin, who cut at Baw-chhun with their knives till he lost consciousness, then slashed at the head and shoulders of the little boy as he clung to his father's legs, and, last of all, made such a furious attack upon the poor blind man, that death must have been almost instantaneous. Meanwhile, Baw-chhun had partially recovered, and was trying to make his escape, when a well-known desperado named Thuh, from Au-soa-thau near Ji-tin, pursued him to the gate of a large house in the village of Kho-siu-tsai. Here a number of persons rushed out, rescued the wounded man, and apprehended his pursuer. Baw-chhun was afterwards sent home in a sedan-chair, and his assailant handed over to the officer in charge at the village of Hoan-sia.

On the following morning, a fruitless search was made for the body of our poor brother, and two of the Christians went to lodge a statement with the county magistrate at Ka-gi city. This latter effort also turned out to be a fruitless one. The two men were simple ignorant country people, they could get no one to put their statement into the proper written form, and the harpies who cluster about the gates of the *Yamen* demanded a heavy bribe before any sort of communication would be taken in.

Afterwards, Tan Tsu-eng the Tsong-ia, or inferior military official at Hoan-a-chhan, arrived in Ka-poa-soa to make investigation; but it soon appeared that the main thing with this person was to have his own expenses very well paid in the first place, while the few inquiries he did make showed that the man Thuh, after being imprisoned for three days at Hoan-sia, made his escape; and that in rushing along, he snatched some clothes belonging to a coolie, who ran after him into a large sugar-store belonging to Gaw-chi-ko. The officer at Hoan-sia has already applied for the recovery of his prisoner, but Gaw-chi-ko refuses to deliver him up. Three other men of this neighbourhood, whose names can be given, are known to have been concerned in the outrage of the 14th. Chiong-hin has returned to Ka-poa-soa, without in any way concealing his guilt, and the serious wounds inflicted on Baw-chhun are still causing much anxiety to all his friends.

Of course, the poor wretched widow of Un Ong was, and still is, in a state of sore distress. She said that her only desire was to have the body of her murdered husband produced, and we are so far relieved to know that this was done in the presence of a large crowd of Christians and heathen on the afternoon of the 20th. It had been dragged for about fifty yards

Murder of Un Ong.

from the place of attack, and then borne away to a place of concealment about a couple of miles off. Six dollars were found in one of the pockets, the skull was battered in on one side, and the whole body covered with frightful gashes. The burial took place that same afternoon.

It would thus seem as if the enemy were determined to dispute with us every inch of ground throughout this Ka-gi region; for, however much those outrages may be the outcome of old anti-Christian feuds, there can be no doubt that the persecutor is abroad at present. Many of the people in Tiam-a-khau hate the light because their deeds are evil, and they can clearly see that Christianity is a cause that 'makes for righteousness' both before God and man. Our earnest prayer is that our dear native brethren may be enabled to show before all that they are now determined to be better neighbours than ever they have been.

12. *Sons of the Prophets.*

TAIWANFOO, 28 *May* 1877.—The training of young men for the native pastorate in Formosa is a subject which has been occupying much of our attention of late. We are fully convinced that any neglect or inefficiency here must, sooner or later, prove fatal to the stability and future extension of the Church.

In the earlier years of the Mission, with few labourers and a rapidly-extending work, it was simply impossible that this department could be attended to as it should, and the result was that many young men were put in charge of stations who had received only a brief and altogether inadequate training in the students' classes at Takow and Taiwanfoo. A proposal made several years ago to send promising lads over to the Theological Seminary at Amoy raised our hopes for a time, but it was soon found that such an arrangement would not work well, and that the Formosa missionaries themselves would require to do the best they could in the circumstances.

We were thus brought lately to the abandonment of Takow as a separate branch of the Mission, and to Taiwanfoo becoming the only centre in Formosa ; a change which has given our students the benefit of almost continuous missionary supervision. Another important addition has been the engagement of a native tutor in the person of Liong-lo, who was baptized at Amoy twenty-three years ago, and is a man whose character and abilities are worthy of all respect. His labours during the past five months have given us much satisfaction, and it is hoped that even greater advance will be made next year, when college buildings are to be erected, with ample teaching and residential accommodation for the brethren engaged in this important department of work.

There are seven students now under training. They attend classes for five hours each day, but their voices may often be heard reading aloud far on into the night. Of course, the missionaries take general superintendence of their studies, giving short simple lectures on Scriptural and other subjects, and conducting the examinations which are held from time to time. For example, they are busy at present in trying to ascertain everything about the origin and contents of the Epistle to the Philippians, and it falls to me on the last day of this month to examine them, both orally and in writing.

The young men are sometimes invited to accompany us on our visits to the more distant stations. The exercise is a very bracing one, and during such intervals, they have capital opportunities for getting acquainted with the practical side of the work to which they are looking forward. I was greatly pleased with the little sermon delivered by one of our students who came with me on a late journey. We arrived on a Saturday at the Taw-kun-eng chapel down south, and Lau-seng was asked to conduct our forenoon service on the following day. He is a Pi-po-hoan from Poah-be, and has been under training for the past three years, but is still a mere lad. His words were addressed to a company of about sixty Christian worshippers, and it was in something like this strain he spoke of 'The race that is set before us':—

'Now,' said he, 'I am very inexperienced, and you must all be asking God to use my weak words for instruction and stimulus, so that every one present may be brought to follow the Lord Jesus more faithfully than ever he has done.

'The *preparation for this race* is what I wish to say a few words about in the first place; for, in order to be a runner here, we must lay aside every weight and the sin which doth so easily beset us. Why, to gain even an earthly prize, it is thought necessary, and men are found willing, to labour and deny themselves. What should we say of the man who had such a contest in view either forgetting all about it, or giving himself up to every indulgence of the passing hour, till the time came when his folly could no longer be concealed or justified? And so we too, brethren, must be up and doing. To run in the way of God's commandments, we must enter in at the strait gate. We must be born again before we can live to the praise and glory of God. Friends, see to it and search your own hearts, lest you may be deceiving yourselves and come short in the end. God's grace is offered to all, but you must ask strength and wisdom to receive it. He is willing to save to the uttermost all who come to Him in the name of Jesus Christ.

'The next thing we have to consider is, *How we are to run the race* set before us; and we do not require to go far for the answer; we must run with patience, looking unto Jesus, the author and the finisher of our faith. Here the Holy Spirit teaches us that God's people must be fully persuaded in their own minds, both as to the great reward prepared for them, and the certainty that, by Divine power, they shall be kept through faith unto salvation. Although their spiritual foes are numerous and crafty and strong, there is no need for serious alarm. They that be with them are more than all their enemies, and the one whose mind is stayed on God may live continually in perfect peace. God's people only require to be diligent in every good work. Their chief concern should be to look unto, to consider, and to imitate the Lord Jesus Christ in all things. He is the only One set before us, and it is to Him alone we should look by faith. Thus looking, we shall be changed into His likeness, and triumph over every obstacle till God shall call us to Himself.

'As to the last particular, *the end of this heavenly race*, How can I find words to speak of it? The Scriptures say, "Eye hath not seen, nor ear heard, neither have entered into the heart of man the things which God hath prepared for them that love Him." In this world the people of

Sons of the Prophets. 427

God cannot hope to escape many trials; nay, because of their faith in Jesus Christ, they may have to pass through greater affliction than many others. But there will be an end to all this. When they have finished their course, they shall obtain rest and an everlasting reward in the kingdom of our Lord. And this reward will not be like an earthly one, for the Apostle Peter says that it is "incorruptible, and undefiled, and fadeth not away." This, then, is what awaits the successful runner we have been speaking of, and this is the reward placed within reach of every one. May all friends here to-day be enabled to choose so good a part!'

The foregoing sentences give a fair, but very incomplete, account of Lau-seng's address, and show nothing at all of the simplicity and unassuming earnestness with which he spoke.

13. *With Brother Pa.*

Taiwanfoo, 1 *June* 1877.—Our senior colporteur, Brother Pa, has just supplied me with notes of a two-months' book-selling and preaching tour in the Chiang-hoa region, from which a few extracts may be given. He made our chapel at Toa-sia his headquarters, always returning there when the heavy rains prevented his travelling about, or when his knapsack again required to have a fresh supply of books.

He states that, on 28th April, he journeyed west to the market-town of Gaw-chhe on the sea-coast, where he met with some little opposition, but also with much encouragement. While he was preaching in the open market-place, a poor drunkard stumbled into the crowd to cause no small disturbance, and one man took the opportunity of stealing a number of his books.

With Brother Pa. 429

In spite of this, however, he managed to sell one hundred and thirty-six little pamphlets and tracts, to have several open-air meetings, and a great amount of conversation with the people in their shops and houses. One scholarly, wealthy-looking man showed a spirit of much friendliness, and another person kindly invited our friend to dinner.

On 1st May he set out for the walled town of Tai-kah, a place where the people are terribly given up to the opium habit, but containing a few who have heard the Gospel, either in Toa-sia or in the Mission Hospital. Here, three men pretended to be greatly interested in what was said, obtained their request for a supply of books, and went away for the money to pay for them, but failed to come back, thus causing a great deal of quiet enjoyment to the people while Pa was kept waiting. After preaching for some time, the proprietor of a respectable grocery shop asked our brother to come and rest himself, on which some of the neighbours gathered round and proposed a great many questions about 'the doctrine'; all of which supplied further opportunity for explaining matters, and exhorting those present to seek salvation through our Lord Jesus Christ. He sold 101 books in Tai-kah.

On 3d May he was off again, this time to the market-town of Pai-a, where, with the exception of some trouble in a pawnshop, into which he had been asked, the people everywhere treated him with kindness, and listened with much attention to his preaching. A poor wretched beggar bought three leaflets. This man seemed to be very much impressed; although, on turning away, there is some reason to think that he re-sold the leaflets for double their value! One decent, intelligent, and sincere-looking woman asked Pa, with much apparent sincerity, if what he had just been saying were really true, and if these books were all about this doctrine. He sold fifty-four books in this place, among them being twenty copies of 'Come to Jesus' translated into Chinese.

From the 7th till the 9th he was engaged in itinerating among a number of villages to the north-east of Toa-sia, besides visiting the towns of Thau-a-ke and Sa-tsap-tiu-le, in the former of which he sold thirty-nine, and in the latter fifty-nine, tracts. He also had large audiences in the open air, and many opportunities for speaking personally to people about 'the things pertaining to the Kingdom.'

On 14th May he went to the thriving town of Tang-si-kak where, among the intelligent Hakka population, he says,

'God set before me an open door, and enabled me to speak the truth with a warm heart.' One hundred and nineteen little pamphlets were sold in this place, fifty-four of these being purchased by a well-to-do man for distribution among his friends and neighbours. An old native doctor, the sign of whose shop is 'Golden Longevity,' was particularly pleased to listen to all that was said, and showed no small kindness to the preacher. That same day he journeyed on to Tang-toa-tun, and here, too, he was strengthened to speak the Word both with love and boldness. In one part of this town a great many persons were busily engaged in gambling, but they were not at all displeased when our brother asked them to hear what he had to say. Their attention was all the greater when Pa began by saying that he was formerly a notorious

With Brother Pa. 433

gambler himself, and guilty of much more wickedness in the sight of God. I well know how it would go on. He would tell them a great deal about himself, past and present. He would have them laughing the one minute, and anxious lest they should lose a word the next. The love and the grace of God working in his own life, and ready now to bring blessing unto them, would be the burden of his message. He cannot but speak of the things he has seen and heard.

There is not a little of the born orator about Brother Pa, and it is something of a treat to watch the provoking good-nature and shrewdness with which he can reply to all objections. I have known him now for six years, and rejoice over him as one who loves the Lord Jesus in sincerity. He does not spare himself in working for the spiritual good of others. We have had many an open-air and indoor meeting together, and his words always impressed me as coming from a man who really believes what he says. He entered our Taiwanfoo chapel one day about seven years ago, when dear old Elder Bun was preaching on the destruction of Sodom and Gomorrah; and, from soon after, having obtained help of God, he has continued unto this day a consistent and most useful servant of the Church.

14. *Baksa New Chapel.*

TAIWANFOO, 17 *July* 1877.—The old chapel at Baksa was put up shortly after my arrival in Formosa. It was a tolerably good building, but the immensely wide tiled roof proved far too heavy for the walls and bamboo rafters; and so, to prevent accident, the entire structure had

Baksa New Chapel. 435

to be taken down some months ago, and arrangements made for the erection of a more substantial one. To carry out this undertaking, the native brethren themselves contributed nearly two hundred dollars, besides manufacturing about twenty thousand sun-dried bricks, and heaping together great quantities of stone, lime, wood, and other necessary materials, the intention being to provide a strong plain building that would comfortably seat not fewer than three hundred persons. The outlying Christian community in the Baksa region far outnumbers this, but the difficulties of travel during the rainy season, with the hope that some of our students may soon be able for work, seem to point in the direction of an early hive-off from the congregation here.

The mason-work must have been pushed forward very rapidly, for a few days ago it was my privilege to conduct our opening services in the new chapel. So far as neatness and solidity are concerned, the building is everything that could be desired. It stands in a field about fifty yards south from the village, and there is still ample room on our ground there for flower-plots, kitchen-garden, schoolroom, and houses for the pastor and teacher. The interior is spacious and very pleasing, the speaker having no pillars or other obstruction before him. The solid brick platform at the east end—about six feet deep and three in height—is tiled on the top, and extends along the whole breadth of the building. A wooden balustrade springs from the outer edge of this platform to a height of three feet or so, within the middle part of which is placed the table with reading-desk, with several long seats on either side for the use of the

Baksa New Chapel. 437

native office-bearers. The floor of the chapel is made of hard cement, and the glass windows and doors are all furnished with strong metal hinges and bolts. The outlay for this work has no doubt been considerable — the Mission's part alone amounting to about nine hnndred dollars —but as this was the third Baksa chapel, we thought it best to have a building that would last for years, and somewhat anticipate a large increase of worshippers from the immediate neighbourhood. The possession of such a place of meeting must be very helpful to the work, and add greatly to the comfort of every one in summer. Of course, our chief desire is that the Lord Himself may consecrate it with His presence, and enable us to say for many a year to come that 'this and that man was born there.'

The brethren commenced to arrive very

early on the morning of our opening day, some coming from Kamana, some from Kongana and Poah-be, and a few from Ka-poa-soa and other more distant churches. There was a good attendance of our local friends, and many heathen who were present ranged themselves on the front and side pavements opposite the doors and windows to regard the whole proceedings with friendly interest. On entering, I felt that the very sight of the hundreds who filled up every part of the spacious lightsome hall was most suggestive, and well fitted to make one think of that scene where 'all the multitude kept silence, and gave audience to Barnabas and Paul, declaring what miracles and wonders God had wrought among the Gentiles.'

I never had my attention so much drawn to the decided change for the better which Christianity is working upon the

Baksa New Chapel. 439

external condition of this people. Instead of the disorder and filth of the old heathen days, we had now before us a cleanly, decently-clad, and well-behaved audience of over four hundred persons, who had come together this beautiful Sabbath morning, not to carry out some great scheme of wickedness, or to yield themselves up to the sins and absurdities of their former idolatry, but for the worship of the living God, and for the praise of Him who had delivered not a few of them from the power of darkness, and translated them into the kingdom of His dear Son. I confess it was only with choking voice I could myself join in with their hearty rendering of the Old Hundredth Psalm. I thought of the time when Dr. Maxwell paid his first visit to this downtrodden people, and felt well assured that all of us had abundant cause to thank God and

take courage. Not that we ourselves have been like angels in carrying on this great work, or that our native brethren, guileless and teachable, are even now simply waiting to be told how they must do the will of God. No; there is not one of our own party but has his weaknesses to speak of before God, while on the Sabbath of which I am now writing, I could see on almost every form, members who had been before the Session for admonishment and rebuke. My meaning is expressed in this sentence from a letter which lately reached me:—
'How much and how little has been accomplished in these years? How little by the Church of God, how much by the Lord of the Church?'

There were everal admissions by baptism at the close of the forenoon service, and in the afternoon about two hundred and fifty members united in partaking of the Lord's Supper. It was, indeed, a memorable day in our history. I felt greatly refreshed in my own soul, and do not remember of ever having spent a more pleasant time with the brethren at this station.

15. Our Hakka Brethren.

TAIWANFOO, 20 *July* 1877.—I have no idea how many Hakka people there may be in Formosa. They are emigrants from the Canton Province, whose dialect differs very much from that of the Amoy-speaking Chinese amongst whom we labour. Many of them are found in the Hong-soa county; and in several parts of Chiang-hoa and Tek-chham, whole towns and villages are occupied by this pushing and intelligent race. The Hakkas compare very favourably with the people around them in the matter of education.

The school is a great institution with them, and all over the country they hold their own in competing for the *Siu-tsai* and *Ku-jin* degrees. They are adherents of the three forms of religion now prevalent in China, but excel their neighbours in greater devotion to the practice of ancestral worship. Their women do not bind the feet, and are always kept very busy in field-work or in marketing.

Mr. Ritchie began work among the Formosan Hakkas a few years ago, his attention being directed then to the village of Lam-gan, about fifteen miles south-east from Takow. At the time of his earlier visits to it, two or three of the better-informed villagers who speak our dialect of Chinese were very friendly, and had no objection to offer when matters were fully explained to them. Indeed, the whole position of things seemed so favourable that my colleague at once engaged a teacher and commenced the study of Hakka. He was much assisted in this linguistic work by a number of Romanised Hakka books from the mainland, while the securing of suitable preaching premises at Lam-gan gave an impetus and visibility to the movement which greatly helped it. We have now a prosperous little congregation there, and the worshippers who attend from other Hakka villages will no doubt use their influence in our favour when the time comes for further extension.

On the evening of a recent visit to Lam-gan, it came on dark before I had reached the end of my journey. I happened to be walking in front of several native brethren at the time, and got thoroughly soused into a deep ditch on our left. The bank here is so very steep that my descent took the form of what some people would call a 'header,' but with no more serious result than a good drenching to myself and much genuine merriment to those who were travelling with me. The little episode had certainly its ludicrous side; for, on being fished out of the green sludge, and appearing before the tired fellows I had been speaking to about the importance of walking 'while ye have the light,' they took such a violent fit of *coughing*, that it was impossible to withhold the sickly smile which set them all off in a roar.

My previous visit to Lam-gan was just about a year ago, and I still remember the generally favourable impression I carried away with me at that time. There were no public scandals to humble us before God, several persons were added to the membership, and a young man was engaged, who has since been holding a good

Our Hakka Brethren. 445

position among our other students in Taiwanfoo.

I feel exceedingly thankful to say that the work here still points in the same encouraging direction. The attendance on Sabbath has considerably increased, and Lam-gan is one of our few stations at which there seems to be something really hopeful about the children's week-day school. I examined ten candidates for baptism, and concluded that seven of these ought to be received into Church membership. My attention was specially drawn to one of them, a boy of fifteen, whose parents are dead, and who lives with his married brother in the neighbouring village of Lau-chhu-tsng. After being at school for about two years, he had to leave at a time when Chinese boys have still to be busy with their primers. The noticeable thing is, that A-ke has plainly made a very good use of the opportunities which God has given him, the evidence of this being his ability to read the Gospel of St. John with fluency, and return intelligent answers on all the leading facts and doctrines of the other New Testament books. It was more, however, the very decidedly favourable testimony of the native office-bearers which opened the way for the admission of this youthful disciple.

The chapel was uncomfortably crowded at both forenoon and afternoon diets of worship. Our respected old native assistant conducted the former in Hakka, and it was at the close of his address that the candidates openly professed their faith by being baptized into the name of the Father, and of the Son, and of the Holy Ghost, One God. May they indeed be enabled to adorn His doctrine by a quiet, consistent, and useful life! This is what tells most upon the masses around us, who, no doubt, listen to our preaching, but have something more to arrest their thoughts when the profligate, thievish, and untruthful are made new creatures in Christ Jesus.

I preached in the afternoon on the mission and work of the Comforter. About fifty united in partaking of the Lord's Supper, their being several brethren present from our church at Tek-a-kha, of which the Lam-gan work may be regarded as an offshoot. I believe that, to many of them, it was truly a season of blessing and refreshment.

16. *Carnival at Ka-gi.*

TAIWANFOO, 21 *July* 1877. — While nearing the city of Ka-gi on a late visit I found the people engaged in their absurd local custom of stone-throwing. This custom began about thirty years ago, and was then confined to the boys of the south gate pelting those of the west with certain kinds of ripe fruit and other harmless missiles. Disputes having arisen, many adults came to the rescue, but only to make matters worse by quarrelling and fighting among themselves; till, like some contagion, the desire to see what was going on, and even to take part in the fray, spread among thousands of the people, who came pouring out from the two gates, and crowding upon that part of the city wall beyond which the boys had been amusing themselves. They were not a little disgusted to learn that the reports of the disturbance were grossly exaggerated. Some of them had come to stand by their friends in the hour of supposed danger; others were ready to engage in a little clan-fighting on their own account; and a few were probably moved with the hope of plunder, but no one was prepared to be told that the whole affair had come to a quiet and sudden collapse. I understand it was then, while the crowds were beginning to disperse, that the westerns—mostly in boisterous fun — commenced throwing small stones at their retiring neighbours of the southern gate, who returned the attack with much spirit, and firmly stood their ground, till darkness and the closing of the city gates compelled them to leave off.

Next morning, large collections of stones and broken tiles were made, challenges were sent from one party to the other, crowds of people again assembled outside the city, and that same afternoon the stone-throwing was resumed with more system, and on a much grander scale than that of the previous day. There were large districts throughout the city where business was quite suspended and the shops closed. The authorities appear to have had no means of checking the disorder, and contented themselves by issuing proclamations to say that no legal redress would be given to persons who might be sufferers in whatever way therefrom; the result being that, for several days, hundreds on hundreds of the people continued to stone each other to their hearts' content. Many of them were seriously wounded, and several deaths were reported; but the curious part of the matter is the spirit of good-natured rivalry which seemed to characterise the entire proceedings; so much so, that persons from the winning side were often seen running over to assist the losing party—thus keeping up the conflict, and just throwing that dash of

Carnival at Ka-gi. 451

hilarity and excitement into the affair, which may have explained the indifference of the mandarins at Taiwanfoo when made aware of what was taking place.

On its anniversary in every succeeding year, the stone-throwing has been renewed by hundreds of people, many of whom seriously regard the practice as being most useful in clearing the atmosphere of evil influences, which would keep lurking about, and ultimately break forth in any amount of injury to life and property. During the quiet Sabbath of my visit at this time, we heard the loud shouting of the crowd beyond the city walls, and the tumult caused by large parties of Yamen officers issuing from the two gates to put forth a weak effort at apprehending the ringleaders. Some one then told me that the prisons were filled with men and lads who had been taken into custody for stone-throwing, but that the County Magistrate was afraid to punish them severely; while his prisoners, so far from being filled with regret or fear for what they had done, appeared to regard themselves as martyrs in the best of causes.

Something of greater interest than any such practices is the fact that the Gospel of the Lord Jesus has now commenced to shine amid the thick darkness of this inland city. All who attend the chapel have quite broken with their former superstitions, take much pleasure in listening to the doctrine, and have shown a commendable amount of forbearance when exposed to petty annoyances on account of their profession. There is good reason to believe that several have really come under the saving influence of the truth.

We are exceedingly hopeful about this Ka-gi work. As nearly all our stations

Carnival at Ka-gi. 453

were in remote little aboriginal villages, the officials and people began to get suspicious of our movements in always passing through crowded Chinese centres to the regions beyond. Extension could not have taken place in a more desirable quarter. Both from position and the number of its inhabitants, Ka-gi naturally ranks as one of the more important counties of Formosa. I have visited a great many of its towns and villages, and can truly say that here, if anywhere, we have a grand opportunity. It is while travelling over it in every direction that one comes to see the immense value of that healing and teaching work which has been quietly carried on for years by the medical members of our Mission. More than once have I spoken to willing listeners and been treated with respect, because of some one who had come under the kindly, skilful treatment of Dr. Maxwell or Dr. Dickson.

While addressing a crowd one day in the district city, a man came forward and warmly invited me to dine with him. He said he could not rest till he came to see me. On inquiry, it turned out that he had formerly been stone-blind, but completely restored to sight through an operation by Dr. Dickson. Now, here was a man who would speak well of us at all hazards; and one who, as a simple matter of fact, went home to his friends and told them how great things the Lord had done for him. By the way, Where is the brother whose heart is fired with ambition of the right sort? Let him become a medical missionary in China. No overcrowding of the profession out here. He'll get a whole Province to himself, with thousands who will shower blessings upon his name. Let no one talk to me about the stolidity and the ingratitude of Chinamen who come under the treatment of an able Christian doctor.

Another thing which may be mentioned in connection with Ka-gi is that, on 31st December last, it was my privilege to baptize a young man from this region who promises very well. Tiau-a was one of the first to stand by us when we took possession of the former little chapel. He continued his attendance for some time, and at last gave up an intention he had of becoming connected with the Buddhist priesthood. I afterwards engaged him as my servant-boy, in which capacity he faithfully served me for more than a year. It was during that time he received admission to the Church, and only some months subsequent to his baptism, we cordially agreed to his becoming one of our theological students. Of course, it is difficult to say much of those who are just beginning their career, but in this case there does seem to be decided cause for hopefulness. Tiau-a has fair average ability, capital health, and I have always found him honest, good-natured, and obedient. We rejoice much that his life gives evidence of having undergone a change which no mere human effort can bring about. We shall watch his progress with much interest. I felt some regret at parting with him, as a good servant in China is almost invaluable, especially to bachelor missionaries.

17. *Evangelising in Sinkang.*

TAIWANFOO, 5 *October* 1877.—Last Sabbath, three of the students and myself had rather a good day at Sinkang, a large

Chinese market-town seven miles northward from Taiwanfoo, and interesting as having been headquarters of the Dutch Mission to Formosa during the first half of the seventeenth century. Many of the present inhabitants were inmates of the Taiwanfoo Hospital at one time or other; and only a few weeks ago, Deacon Bi of Baksa visited the place, when the Thong-su—or Chief of the colony of civilised aborigines still resident here—with quite a number of his neighbours, expressed a desire to know something more of this new 'Saviour-Lord doctrine.'

It would be about six o'clock when we issued from the great north gate. The morning was cloudy, yet delightfully fresh and cool, enabling us to dispense entirely with the usual sun-spectacles and umbrella. What a heavy dew we have in Formosa here! and how very inspiring the thought as we now left the city that, as the dew of Hermon, and as the dew that descended upon the mountains of Zion, so, before noon that day, the rich blessing of our gracious God would be descending upon this beloved land of our adoption! Barclay was away in the thick darkness of the Ka-gi region; Smith, some fifty miles further south at Takow; our worthy Doctor, assisted by the senior colporteur and others, were ready for action at Taiwanfoo; while in the far north, Mackay and Frazer, with their band of well-trained preachers, would also be waiting to see another day of the Son of Man.

We seldom halted by the way, and reached Sinkang just as a party of over thirty travelling play-actors entered the town to prepare for a great torchlight performance, which was to be held here that same evening. They certainly seemed to have the advantage of us so far as outward appearances go. A large awning had been put up in front of one of the temples; there were dresses, and weapons, and other such articles in abundance; and one could easily see that the people were only too eager to become spectators of the idolatrous and unholy entertainment. But, knowing that the Lord of Hosts was upon our side, we did not hesitate long. Weak and timid enough in ourselves, we looked up, and, like Abraham's servant of old, breathed a silent prayer that God would send us good speed that day, and use our poor words for the enlightenment of those sitting in this region and shadow of death.

A crowd had already commenced to follow us, which increased at almost every step as we wended our way through the busy market-place, on to a wide vacant piece of ground where we halted to commence our work. As a matter of course, all sorts of questions and suggestions were proposed as to the object of our visit, some thinking we had merely stopped on our way to the north, and that our chairs and luggage were following on behind; others that we had come to practise the healing art; a few that we were here from one of the *Hongs*, or European warehouses, to seek new openings for trade, and so on. They appeared to be quite satisfied when I told them we had no such object in view, but were now amongst them to speak about the true God, and the way they could all become possessed of lasting happiness—a statement which brought one face to face with the exceeding difficulty of addressing a Chinese heathen audience on the truths of Scripture.

In the first place, their minds keep in-

Evangelising in Sinkang. 461

cessantly active on matters having not the slightest reference to the subject of discourse; and then, when they do pay some attention, it is only to fall into all sorts of mistakes as to the meaning of one's imperfectly spoken words. On this occasion we tried to be as short and pointed in our addresses as possible, each speaker confining himself to the statement and illustration of one particular point at a time. I made as good a commencement as I could by trying to explain about there being only one living and true God, who was everywhere present, who knew all things, was holy, merciful, and good to all His creatures, and who would ultimately reward every man according to his works. There were several interruptions while I spoke, a somewhat officious individual always wishing to come in as a kind of interpreter by saying that it was

'Thi-kong' I was exhorting the people to worship—this 'Thi-kong' being only a high-class deity of their own creation.

One of the students followed with a very homely and practical address on man's sin against God, as shown in failing to acknowledge Him, in worshipping idols, and in the misery seen everywhere around us. The awful curse of Formosa having been referred to—opium-smoking —a person took occasion to remark that it was our foreign country in which the opium was cultivated. His meaning was that there would have been no opium-smokers among the Chinese had foreigners not first supplied them with the drug. In such a case I find it best, as a rule, simply to say that we do greatly regret to know that a few of our countrymen are engaged in the trade, but that this fact in no way exonerates them from the sin and folly

Evangelising in Sinkang. 463

of using opium as they do. The explanations are generally received in very good part; but it is almost impossible for one to overcome a feeling of shame in thinking of our countrymen as being so largely accountable for flooding China with an article whose hopeless victims, even in Formosa, can now be numbered by tens, if not hundreds, of thousands. We remained here about two hours, preaching and conversing with a company of people who questioned some of our statements, and wished to inquire about several things we had been saying. At the close, from thirty to forty small Christian books were readily disposed of.

We then moved away in the direction of the temple where the before-mentioned play-actors had taken up their quarters, to find that nearly all of them were busy gambling in front of the idols. I tried to say a few words to the people who came after us, but the confusion was too great; so that we came down again to the market-place, had a little refreshment at one of the stalls there, and afterwards took up our stand in front of a large unoccupied building, the covered awning before which served as a very grateful shade from the fierce heat of the mid-day sun. It was especially in this place I was made to feel that our visit had not been altogether in vain. Not that there was anything striking in the way of people confessing their sins, or receiving the doctrine as something they had long been in search of. No; the Chinese mind is most terribly carnal, and slow, slow to move towards things that are spiritual. I just mean that at this second place we were enabled to speak with more liberty than before, our audience also being a little more intelligent and appreciative-looking than the one we had at the other end of the town. Our sale of books, too, was brisker,—so much so, indeed, that the demand soon exceeded our small supply.

It was well on in the afternoon before we started again for Taiwanfoo, which was reached just a little before dark, all of us feeling that now, with more missionaries and students in the City than heretofore, Sinkang might well come in for an occasional preaching-visit without much weakening of our hands in the other more regular work.

18. *The Highways and Hedges.*

TAIWANFOO, 22 *February* 1878.—Our evangelistic work in Formosa is very much confined to opportunities which present themselves while visiting the out-stations.

It is certainly to be regretted that this important duty of carrying out the words of the Great Commission should occupy so subordinate a place, but the labourers with us are few, while the pastoral and educational work to which we already stand committed takes up so much of our time, that it is difficult to see how matters could well be otherwise. Occasionally, we do arrange for preaching-work in towns and villages off the beaten track, and during the opening days of the Chinese New Year, we always try to get out by the highways and hedges of the region beyond. No other time of the year is more favourable for such work. For twelve months, the people everywhere have been engaged in one incessant grind at their worldly occupations, but on the last night of the twelfth moon, young and old all over the Empire call a halt, and

The Highways and Hedges. 467

spend the few succeeding days in visiting, in pleasure-seeking, and in idling about. They will then gather round in great numbers and leisurely listen to our message. No doubt, many of them devote the holidays to gambling and the opium-pipe, but others allow better counsels to prevail, and come out to wait upon us for hours at a time.

The preaching tour from which I returned a few days ago was very interesting, and showed both the need for such work and the beneficial effect it has upon all who take part in it. A few of the native brethren accompanied me, and we left the city unfettered with any engagement, and very much in ignorance as to where we might spend the nights. A crowd of about two hundred persons assembled in the market-town of Oan-nih, to whom a hundred and ninety leaflets were sold, and the Word preached from the steps of one of the temples. We halted also for more than an hour in Tiam-a-khau, and endeavoured to show many in this town of ill repute that, except they repented, there was nothing for them but to perish in their sins.

One is often put to sore straits in thus labouring among purely heathen audiences. The people are wholly in darkness regarding the Scripture definition of sin; they know nothing of God, or of holiness, or heaven, or hell, or of any one distinctively Christian truth. We speak to them of the true Siong-te or God, and they at once conclude that reference is made to one of their own divinities; of sin, and they tell you that they are not a bad people; of the immense blessedness of being saved, and some anxious soul will ask what you paid for your coat, and how many dollars you get a month for going about preaching in this way. Amid all discouragements, however, we often feel strengthened in recalling the command and the promise of our ascended Lord. Besides, the joy has already been given us of seeing some from among this carnally-minded people made living epistles of Christ Jesus, and it is the belief that this will take place again and again, which renders our work not only bearable, but, of all others, the most pleasant.

From the city of Ka-gi we made a short journey to Thaw-khaw, a town where one of our party—Brother Tiau-a, from the missionary college at Taiwanfoo—was previously well known, and where he renewed some old friendships among people who knew him before he became a Christian, about three years ago. We reached Thaw-khaw on Wednesday afternoon, and the most superficial observer could not but notice the improved appearance of the place and people as compared with other Chinese and aboriginal towns. It was really very remarkable to miss everywhere the long array of gambling-tables at this time of the year. There seemed to be no occupation of the kind going on at all; and on inquiry, it turned out that Tan Toa-lo, the local mandarin, was one who exercised the strictest discipline upon all offenders who were brought before him. Opium-smoking was sternly discouraged, and he simply would not tolerate gambling on any condition.

Being somewhat off the main north road, Europeans seldom visit this town, so that curiosity must have been the leading motive which influenced the large crowds in following us. On telling them we had come to preach to them, they cried out that the largest temple was unoccupied, that if we went there they could both hear better, and we should be out of the way of interrupting other people. To this temple, therefore, we went, and in less than half an hour there met before us an audience which our senior colporteur characterised as being the largest and best behaved he had ever addressed in Formosa. The temple-keeper kindly brought out a bench, and on this we alternately stood while speaking to the dense crowd which filled up every part of the first court.

I think that the three of us who addressed them received the aid of God's Holy Spirit, and it was most delightful to witness the entirely manful yet modest way in which Tiau-a was enabled to speak. It had been his first visit to the place since he left Ka-gi, more than three years ago. He was then a poor ignorant lad, and one who had no hope of rising above the position of an ordinary coolie or petty hawker; one, too, who was both pitied and hated for having consented to the invitation of the foreigner that he should come for training to Taiwanfoo. Indeed, some of the people there seriously believed that we had made away with Tiau-a, and that there was no likelihood of his ever being seen again. In spite, however, of all their absurd rumours, Tiau-a was here among them once more; and although he had departed for a season, it would be difficult to think, either in looking at his neat, genteel appearance, or in listening to the brave, earnest words he spoke, that the Church was an institution for harming people, or leading them to have hearts like beasts, as some of the Chinese are said really to believe.

Brother Pa, the senior colporteur, also

spoke with much freedom, his address occupying fully more than an hour. It was while noticing the effect which their words produced, that I felt increasingly the importance of having a band of well-trained natives to assist us in our work. Oh that we had even one such man stationed in every town and village of the island! There was so much noise and confusion at the close of the meeting, that we had to give up all thought of engaging in colporteur work, the people being quietened only when told that we would remain with them a day longer, and give them a further opportunity of hearing the doctrine and obtaining copies of our publications. We accordingly had three large open-air meetings on Thursday, when about five hundred tracts were readily purchased.

Ka-gi was reached on Friday, but the

city was in such a state of commotion on the following day, that we were compelled to remain indoors. It appeared that a Buddhist saint had advertised far and near that he would publicly ascend a ladder of knives, and this so-called meritorious act it was my lot to witness. The ladders were each about eighty feet high, and had steps made of large sword-like knives. There were thousands upon thousands of people present, whose great desire seemed to be to catch some of the small printed leaves the sorcerer threw from the little platform where the upper ends of the two ladders nearly met. I was told afterwards that, before coming out, his Saintship had taken the precaution to have many plies of hard thin paper pasted on the soles of his feet. He made a pretence of enduring great pain, and the people seemed to think that they were in the presence of one who possessed an extraordinary amount of superfluous merit.

I returned to Taiwanfoo by the main road, and then also had good opportunities for wayside preaching.

19. *A Visit to the Ka-le.*

TAIWANFOO, 10 *May* 1878.—Ka-le is the Chinese name applied to the uncivilised tribes occupying the south-eastern part of Formosa, and I have just returned from a visit to several of their villages. It was during the course of my recent stay at Lam-gan I found that the mother of the Elder there belonged to one of those tribes, and that he himself was familiar with their language and customs. The information he gave me regarding them only whetted my desire to ascertain personally how far they differed from the tribes I lately visited in the mountain region eastward from Chiang-hoa. It happened, too, that I had then a few spare days on hand before going on for the Communion services at Tek-a-kha ; and, accordingly, with the preacher from this station, and a good sturdy native as burden-bearer, I started shortly after daybreak on the morning of 25th *ult.*

The hills stand out well towards the west in the neighbourhood of Lam-gan, but it required a stiff walk of fully five hours before we reached the point at which our climbing commenced. While still a good way off, it was with some surprise we saw a great crowd of natives in front of us, who were shouting and hurrying about in rather an alarming way. There were no villages at hand, and no way of escape from being mixed up in what seemed to be a serious clan-fight. On coming up, however, we were relieved to find only a mob of active Chinamen eagerly engaged in bartering with the savages, who, sure enough, were now to be seen with loads of charcoal, firewood, skins, and other such commodities. Considerable delay was caused by the barterers spreading the report that we wished to go inland only for the purpose of injuring the people, and it was not till a small reward was offered that several stalwart Ka-le undertook to lead us to their settlement at Ka-piang—an arrangement which suited very well, as this place was said to be the residence of a chief who rules over eighteen of the surrounding villages.

Soon after, we were toiling up the side of a very high hill, from the summit of which a most magnificent view was obtained. The plains away towards the west appeared to be one immense rice-field, broken only by occasional clumps of tall feathery bamboos; while, on before, the great wooded mountains rose range upon range, as far as the eye could reach. Our guides said that a commencement had been made in the cultivation of tea in this region, and that those hillsides yielded them fine yearly crops of millet, tobacco, and sweet potatoes. About an hour before sunset, we halted on another ridge in view of Ka-piang, a lovely village in the midst of glorious scenery, and where we were to have the unspeakable joy of telling the inhabitants the story of redeeming love for the first time.

We no sooner entered the village than the cleanliness and appearance of rough material comfort on every side arrested our attention. The houses are built of stone, and tiled with huge slabs of a slaty

A Visit to the Ka-le. 479

kind of rock often met with in central Formosa; while inside, they all seemed nicely fitted up with accommodation for sleeping, and cooking, and storing up articles for household and personal use. The people themselves were found to be a finely-made, healthy-looking race, their faces free from tattoo-marks, and all of them wearing a reasonable amount of clothing—not a few, indeed, being rather prettily arrayed in bright-coloured dresses, and ornamented with earrings, bangles, and necklaces of cornelian stone.

Of course we were at once conducted to the residence of the chief—a long, low, substantially-built stone house on the left, with betel-nut palms in front, and a wide paved court, into which had gathered a very eager and expectant crowd. Another noticeable building we passed was the storehouse or granary for preserving the common stock of rice, millet, taro, and sweet potatoes; our attention being also called to a spacious stone platform under the spreading branches of a great four-trunked banyan, and which the natives said was used as the Judgment-place, or general palaver-house, of the village.

I have referred to the chief, but was hardly prepared for a couple of stately-looking dames coming forth to welcome us in that capacity. It appears that in south Formosa it is no uncommon thing to have women acting as chiefs and village-elders, an arrangement I do not remember to have met with among any of the northern tribes, but one which seems to work here to the satisfaction of all concerned. The two women who now welcomed us were sisters, had bright intelligent faces, and were quite evidently accustomed to receive the respectful obedience of the

A Visit to the Ka-le.

people around them. As already stated, their rule extends to eighteen other villages; although it should be observed that, in addition, each of those villages has its own resident headman or headwoman, as the case may be.

Messengers having been sent on before to announce our approach, the natives were there in strong force, and at the critical moment of introduction, as well as during our subsequent speechifying and interviews on more serious matters, the linguistic aid of an old Chinese-speaking villager was found to be most helpful. The proceedings of the first half-hour were somewhat interesting, and conducted with an amount of ceremony I was scarcely prepared for, one influential man after another rising to assure us of their friendship and hospitality. The clear musical ring of their language was also very pleasing, and immediately suggested a resemblance between it and the dialect spoken by our Sek-hoan brethren in the north; although the remark was afterwards made that people from the two regions speaking to each other would be mutually unintelligible.

I tried to get through my own part of the ceremony by making a statement in Chinese to the effect that all present were children of the one great Father—that I had often heard of their beautiful country, and now appeared amongst them as a true friend—that the land I came from was far from this, but some of the people there often thought of them, and desired that they should obtain the help and blessing of Him who dwelt away up in those beautiful skies—that it was God who dwelt in that glorious place—that He was our Father, who knew us all, and wished all to be His own people—and so on.

A Visit to the Ka-le. 483

The elder of the two sisters was here understood to say that I was very welcome; that there were few things in their poor place to attract me, but they would do everything they could to make me comfortable. I then again endeavoured to convey to those willing listeners a few of the simpler truths of the Bible, and felt much encouragement in doing so from the close attention which was paid, and the hearty expressions of approval which greeted every statement from our useful interpreter.

At length a few of our presents were produced, including about twelve yards of a highly-coloured cotton print, which at once called forth the admiration and joy of every one present. It was a piece of the flimsiest Manchester stuff, with great staring flowers on a frightful pattern of scroll-work; and yet that bit of cloth produced a remarkable impression on the minds of those people. All formality was now banished; I was looked upon as having had some share in the manufacture of this wonderful production; the word was passed that a first-class medicine-man had come amongst them; and their pent-up feelings found expression in the issue of an order to have supper prepared forthwith.

Later on there was even a larger meeting than the former one, and here again I tried to make good use of Ku-a-mih, the interpreter. The advance was made this time of telling them about prayer to God, and of how our voices were to be used in singing His praise. They greatly relished the Po-sia tunes, which were sung to several of our sweet little Chinese hymns. These had to be repeated time after time, the native music being more intelligible to them than any specimens from our home collection. We did not retire that even-

A Visit to the Ka-le. 485

ing till nearly midnight, and I shall long remember the occasion as being a time when God enabled us to make substantial acknowledgment of the unaffected kindness of this people.

While moving about the following morning, my eye caught sight of a village across the ravine, and beautifully situated on the brow of a hill south-east from Ka-piang. It seemed populous, too, and the journey there and back to be a matter of very easy accomplishment. On asking for a guide to go over with me, the people at once raised many objections, and said it would never do for me to go wandering about. They added that the road was longer than I imagined; that the inhabitants were not on friendly terms with them; that I would not get anything to eat there, and that no one was present who would be willing to accompany me.

As their manifold reasons against going only increased my interest in this village of Pun-tih, I very willingly faced the task of persuading them a little, with the result that in about an hour after I was fairly on the way. The preacher and an experienced old native came with me, and we had gone but a very little distance, when it was found that they had certainly made no exaggeration about the steepness and roughness of the road. We went scrambling and sliding down, down; and any narrow platform we did reach seemed but the commencement of a yet more difficult stage of the journey. About half-way up the side of the opposite hill, a curious kind of stone enclosure containing the skulls of murdered Chinamen arrested our attention. It must be understood that the natives here conform to the practice of head-hunting. On the very

A Visit to the Ka-le. 487

morning of the day I am now writing about, I pointed with strong disapprobation to a broken-in skull before several of the Ka-piang villagers, but they immediately and with great emphasis shouted out, *Lang-wah! Lang-wah!* meaning that all their customs in connection with the practice of head-hunting were not only blameless, but greatly to be commended.

After all, there was not very much to reward us at this village of Pun-tih; less, no doubt, than if we had been accompanied by our useful old interpreter. The resident chief here also is a woman, a young person who, when called for, came out and modestly sat down at some little distance; the men and children gathering round in a large crowd and giving us every assistance they could. I wrote down a number of their words. It seems evident that a close bond of connection runs through all the widely differing aboriginal languages of Formosa,—so much so, that an intimate knowledge of one would furnish a key for the very easy acquisition of any other, and even itself be of service for communicating with many thousands of the people.

High as the village of Pun-tih stands —of Ka-piang, too, for that matter—it was pleasant to observe the abundance of clear, cool water with which the inhabitants were supplied. We relished it all the more on this occasion, because there was no attempt at supplying us with anything more substantial, the hint being dropped that, having come empty-handed, the chief and her counsellors thought it best to discountenance so objectionable a precedent by withholding all commissariat supplies. They could not, however, prevent one from feasting on the truly grand scenery away in every direction from their

A Visit to the Ka-le.

picturesque little village; and one thing more, they could not hinder us from seeing two other snug little hamlets away on the other side, and within only a pleasant walk from our headquarters at Ka-piang.

As little could be done in the way of speaking to the people, an immediate return was agreed upon. We felt very hungry, had once more to go down the one side and up the other of that great inevitable V, while another evening among the people at Ka-piang seemed to be an important item in turning my few days' sojourn to most account.

Our friends gladly welcomed us back again, and spoke in rather a complimentary way on the rapidity with which we had performed our short, though somewhat difficult, journey. I expressed my desire to visit about a little more, and was pleased to see that no further objections were raised; that, on the contrary, virtue was made of a necessity, and an arrangement come to that the head of the tribe herself, with Ku-a-mih and a number of young braves, should accompany me on a visit to the two villages we had seen from the other side.

Meanwhile, a number of hours still remained of that Tuesday, and I resolved to devote at least a part of the time to making out a short vocabulary of the words made use of by this people. A stone seat under the banyan was chosen; five or six boys with a little knowledge of Chinese drew near; old Ku-a-mih was within call; every one was willing to help, and the work soon proved to be both a pleasant and an easy one to all concerned. As in Malay, the 'a' sound predominates very largely in their speaking; and, although

A Visit to the Ka-le. 491

many of the words they use are quite differently pronounced, there could be no mistaking the general resemblance of the language to that spoken by our Po-sia brethren, and by the savages living further east from them. On this head, and taking into account some facts collected during a recent visit to the Ku-a-lut aborigines at South Cape, I should say that with very little extra work, a knowledge of the language spoken by any one of those native tribes would be everywhere available on the eastern side of the island, and turn out to be by far the readiest way of gaining the confidence of the people. Surely what took place on Pentecost implies that the Church should declare unto all men the wonderful works of God, *in their own tongue.* Indeed, without this power of speech, no kind of improvement can be effected among a people like Formosan aborigines. The plan now being tried by the authorities of opening schools, and imparting to them a knowledge of Chinese, has not been successful, the words being difficult to pronounce, the characters an entire mystery, and the lads very frequently obviating all further trouble by running off again to their wild and roving life among the hills.

By the way, it is quite impossible not to like the nice, frank, healthy-looking children one meets with in these eastern villages. They have much of the fun, a great deal of the intelligence, and all the naturalness and faith, of English boys. How they did laugh at my mistakes that evening while writing down their words! And what a time we had while I scattered among them the contents of five small confection bottles! I suppose the fine little fellows would have gone anywhere

A Visit to the Ka-le.

with me; the grown-up people were compelled to be good-natured, and our visit will no doubt form a subject of remark for many a day to come.

It was on the evening of the second day that a general muster for worship took place, the few who made up our own party beginning with the Chinese version of 'From Greenland's icy mountains,' and then thanking God for bringing us here, and asking that the light of the knowledge of salvation through Jesus Christ might soon dispel the darkness of this place. An attempt was afterwards made to convey one or two of the more leading doctrines of the Bible, our little friends meanwhile looking up with their big, trustful, wondering eyes, and the adults uttering an occasional expression of approval as our interpreter tried 'to give the sense and cause them to understand' the meaning. They seemed again to be very much taken with the praise part of our worship, on which I sang 'The Lord's my Shepherd,' and ' The sands of time are sinking,' although it was mostly through the hymns from our own Chinese collection we endeavoured to interest and instruct them.

On the following morning we started to visit the two villages seen from Puntih, the nearest of which, they told us, was Tu-kuh-vul, and the other, about half a mile further on, Ku-la-lutch. The preacher remained behind, myself and servant-boy being accompanied by the head of the tribe, the interpreter, and several followers, with a small armed party acting as a guard of honour. I remember one time looking round to see the rather handy — if somewhat undignified and primitive—style of locomotion adopted

A Visit to the Ka-le.

by the honourable one of our party. A sturdy fellow had brought with him a long continuous band or ring of cloth—hide, perhaps it was—one end of which was placed over the front part of his head, and the other, dangling from behind, made to serve as a support for the knees of her Chieftainship, who was thus simply being carried along upon the man's back, looking as erect, and trying to feel as comfortable, as one could do in her rather *uncanny* position. I may add that the dress of this aboriginal lady was appropriately much finer in material, and more tasteful in form, than that of the other female villagers ; another of her marks of distinction being the long knife or dagger which hung from her side, and the wooden sheath of which was beautifully ornamented with a profusion of brass scroll-work. On coming within sight of Tu-kuh-vul, several guns were fired off to announce our arrival. I happened to be walking in front at the time, and was the first to meet the villagers who came out to bid us welcome. The one who seemed to be the leader of this party was truly a stout fine-looking man, head of the village, as they afterwards told me, and none other than the husband of my hostess. He wore a very glossy leopard's-skin coat or long jacket, which was furnished with a number of little brass bell-like ornaments, so arranged that a perpetual, though not unpleasant, jangling sound accompanied him in all his movements.

Like our Ka-piang friends, the people here also seem to be tolerably well off in a worldly sense, there being, at least, no doubt as to the frank and liberal way in which they treated us on the present occasion. In the chief's house a large—shall

I say distinguished?—party met, nearly all of them intent on doing justice to the huge bowlfuls of steaming soup, the junkets of fat pork, the sweet potatoes, and the not unpalatable kind of millet porridge, on which those villagers may be said to live and thrive. All this indoors, while outside—and still in our honour, I suppose—the most prominent feature appeared to be a pretty general sort of tippling in weak spirits which was briskly going forward among the men. I observed they made use of a peculiar cup, or rather two cups carved out of one long piece of wood, so that two persons might drink close together at the same time. From anything I saw or could learn, I don't think they are at all what one would call a drunken people. We did not remain long after dinner, but went on to Ku-la-lutch, a somewhat larger village than the other one; and where, too, the people treated us in a very friendly and respectful way.

Our brief stay here was spent under one of the trees overshadowing the stone platform or palaver-ground, where some fifty or sixty of the villagers soon collected, and commenced proceedings by inviting me to partake of a yellowish brose-like compound I thought it safest to decline; but which, with much apparent relish, was speedily drunk or eaten up, as one might say, by the male portion of the grown-up people. It appeared that when we arrived, the discovery was made of there being no supply of native spirits on hand wherewith to make merry; so that, rather than omit this mark of native hospitality, they had resolved on using the contents of the great round jar before us. It contained a wet mass of the millet before referred to in the earlier stages of fermentation; suitable

A Visit to the Ka-le. 499

enough as raw material for the purpose intended, but certainly neither safe nor pleasant in its present state; and yet, it was remarkable the extent to which some of the older hands be-slobbered themselves.

On returning to Ka-piang, it was found that a considerable number of people had come together in view of our departure the following morning; among them being a few from Tu-kuh-vul whom we met with in the earlier part of the day. We had more singing, and further attempts to enlighten them as to the great object of our visit. I said they should pray that, before long, some one might come and teach them all to become the true people of God. They should not go on as they had been doing. God knew everything, and was very much grieved when they did wrong. He was willing, however, to pardon their sins if they only asked Him, for Jesus' sake, to do so. Jesus, as I had already been telling them, was the best and truest Friend we ever had, or could have. If they only trusted in Jesus, all would go well with them. They need not fear anything then. Jesus would lead them at last to heaven. Heaven was a good place, and they should all ask Jesus to lead them there.

Of course, it was impossible for me to know the exact nature of the change which such simple sentences underwent when interpreted by Ku-a-mih, while we were still more in the dark as to what conception his words gave rise in the minds of these poor benighted brethren of mankind. We could only feel thankful they all remained so quiet, and appeared in a kind of general way to follow the drift of our meaning. Alas! one's helplessness even with all appliances! May the Lord, indeed, by His own gracious Spirit soon find a way of bringing them to the saving knowledge of Himself!

Before breaking up that evening, several of them presented me with a few small tokens of remembrance, including one of the before-mentioned drinking-cups, a large knife with ornamental sheath from the chief of Tu-kuh-vul, a rudely carved wooden box, with a number of smaller articles from some of the younger people. My presents had already been made, but I took occasion to round-off this part of the business by presenting our Tu-kuh-vul friend with a brightly-coloured coverlet, on the centre of which was wrought a large representation of the British crown. By signs and otherwise, I explained that this was the distinctive decoration of our beloved Chief; at which he smiled, and seemed to think that he, too, had now obtained something that would command the respect of those around him.

We were up betimes the following morning, and had a good walk over before the sun appeared from the top of the hills behind us, our first real halt being at that bartering-place I referred to on the inward journey. We rested here for about an hour, during which the crowd of petty traders who were present came eagerly about, wishing to know all the particulars of our reception by the natives, and whether we really thought that gold and other valuables existed among them, many Chinese having still the belief that on such a journey even we could have nothing else in view than to ' *chhu po*,' or search for precious things. As the bustle of the day had not yet commenced, and the preacher with me could make himself intelligible to the Hakka portion of them, we took our stand on the top of a large stone, and almost immediately had a tolerably good audience before us, listening to our feeble account of Him with whom 'all the things that may be desired are not to be compared.' O the privilege of being His ambassadors in such a cause! The preacher spoke with a great amount of pointedness and freedom.

Resuming our journey, it was not long before we reached our Lam-gan station, which had been the starting-point for the expedition.

20. *Declension at Tek-a-kha.*

TAIWANFOO, 15 *May* 1878.—Tek-a-kha is a Chinese village about ten miles south-east from Takow, in which Christian work has been carried on during the past six or seven years. At first the movement was greatly indebted to the influence of a military graduate of the place, whose sincere profession of discipleship led many of the poorer people to become interested in the truth. The present condition of things will be seen from the following notes of my late visit to this station.

I arrived on a Saturday afternoon, and at once began the examination of several candidates for baptism, who were all somewhat unresponsive, and had little that could be said either for or against them in the matter of their daily conduct. It is in dealing with people of this class we often have much difficulty in knowing the precise course to take. Any answers they do give show some familiarity with the saving truths of Scripture; there is nothing positively blameworthy in their lives, and here they are of their own accord applying for admission to the Church of Christ. It is very evident that one must either accede to their request, or have some reasonable account to give for keeping them back. Not that one is able in every case just to place the finger, so to speak, on the answer or that particular part of the conduct which not only justifies, but enjoins, our refusal. There is a great deal in a man's appearance and manner, and much may be learned of his present movements from the light of the past. Moreover, surely no one will attempt to fix the extent to which the Spirit of God may help us while sitting with those candidates. In short, we need to remember that our responsibility here does not end by taking care lest hypocrites and the sinfully ignorant be received, but reaches also to the danger of closing the way against those for whom Baptism and the Lord's Supper are more especially intended. A table is spread for the hungry, and it is the weak who claim most of our kindness and attention. On this occasion, I could see my way to receive only Brother Thiok, and one woman who had been a worshipper for some time, but whose Christian character was said to be very much in advance of her knowledge of Scripture.

After our examinations, the native preacher came to me about a certain matter. He said that since the death of the only elder and deacon of the congregation he was feeling very much alone, uncomfortable in having the Church's small income and outlay in his hands, and conscious of his own weakness in visiting among the people, or when any little business required to be done; 'Would it not therefore be well that Ui-jin should be appointed to the deaconship to-morrow?' I told him there was certainly nothing wrong in his proposal; that, on the contrary, we all sympathised with him and would do anything we could to strengthen his hands. As to this Ui-jin, everything I knew or could ascertain about him was decidedly favourable. He was baptized several years ago by Mr. Ritchie, and up till now had borne the character of a sincere, well-behaved, quiet kind of a man, and one who had all along been most exemplary in the matter of Church attendance. The result was that I agreed to appoint him should the brethren unanimously desire it—a mode of procedure which may have a good deal of unpresbyterian haste about it, but which is simply unavoidable in a place where the harvest is ripe and the labourers are few.

The congregation on Sabbath morning was much thinner than we had been accustomed to see at this station; but considerable attention was shown, and one felt encouraged to go on from the careful-like way in which three or four brethren turned up a number of passages which had been referred to. . After the baptisms, only a very short statement was required in the matter of Ui-jin's election. I said they all knew the need there was for having the vacant offices filled up; and that, meanwhile, the appointment even of one to act as deacon would help the Church and prepare the way for something better. I added that Ui-jin had been spoken of by some of us as eligible for this office, but they must remember that the election rested wholly with themselves; so that I would now retire to the sitting-room to give any member an opportunity for stating objections, or suggesting the name of some other brother to fill the office. After an interval of about half an hour, a few of them came to say that there were no objections, that no other name could be suggested, and that all of them would gladly welcome the appointment of Ui-jin. Seeing that arrangements had been made for our Communion in the afternoon, I just detained them a little longer and proceeded with his formal designation to office. It was a very simple service, and included the reading of relevant portions of Scripture, with suitable remarks, our brother's affirmative reply to the questions which were asked, giving of the right hand of fellowship, a short address to the people on the duties which they now had undertaken, and the whole concluding with prayer, praise, and the benediction. We had a pleasant meeting in the afternoon. About thirty of us sat down at the table of the Lord, and to some at least it was a time which recalled that word spoken by the disciple of old, 'Did not our heart burn within us while He talked with us by the way, and while He opened to us the Scriptures?'

During my subsequent stay with the brethren here, I was grieved to find that Church matters with them are not by any means in what can be called a prosperous way. It seems that the Sabbath attendance has considerably fallen off, while hardly any one is found willing to come near the chapel for instruction throughout the week. It should no doubt be borne in mind that the Tek-a-kha people are very poor, and dependent for a livelihood on their daily work, which usually begins at daybreak and lasts on till late in the afternoon. Another thing is that, as a rule, they are quite unable to read or write—even the few educated among them

Declension at Tek-a-kha.

having sometimes the greatest difficulty in deducing anything like sense out of those Chinese characters they are able to name so glibly. With these facts before us, it is obvious that in all our dealings with such brethren we cannot but attach a very special value to their diligent attendance on the means of grace.

It need hardly be said that these people occupy a very different position from worshippers at home, where church-going comes in very much as a mere matter of course, and where not only the opportunities, but the positive inducements to a life of progress in the knowledge of Christ may be said to hedge one round on every side. Take the very ordinary case of Brother Thiok, who was baptized on the occasion of this visit. He is a man of some thirty years of age, unable to read, and earning a livelihood as partner in a little grocery business in the village of Khe-chiu, about a couple of miles distant from Tek-a-kha. Now, supposing this man to be insincere in his profession, all one can say is that, considering the pressure under which it is maintained, this state of things cannot last very long. Either the preaching of the Gospel will be made to him the savour of life unto life, or he will fail to obtain the worldly good he looked for, become disappointed, and end by going back again to his old heathenish practices and beliefs. On the other theory, that Thiok has indeed 'obtained mercy of the Lord,' surely his position in that village, and his whole after-course, as one who has been called and chosen, become invested with no slight amount of interest. One wishes then to know how he stands affected towards the services at Tek-a-kha, since irregularity here cannot be made up by intercourse with villagers who think it wrong for any Chinaman to become a Christian, or by merely possessing the Chinese Bible, which is of the same use to him as a copy of the Septuagint would be to some ignorant labourer.

And as with individuals, so with those poor uneducated and scattered little congregations. The loss which they sustain by absenting themselves from public worship becomes at once apparent; just as their appreciative waiting on the means of grace—because frequently kept up under circumstances of peculiar difficulty—brings with it any amount of blessing to them, being both the earnest and the accompaniment of all true spiritual progress.

As to our congregation at Tek-a-kha, one cannot forget that the recent death, first of the only elder and then of the only deacon, has had rather a depressing effect upon both members and adherents. The former office-bearer was a remarkably active man, and occupied some inferior position in the military service of the district. He spent much of his time in visiting among the brethren, and I was greatly pleased to hear of his constant willingness to go and pray with those who were in sickness. I should not be at all surprised if some of the worshippers have forsaken us on the deliberate conviction that there could be no good luck attending a movement which was deprived of its leaders in this way. The Chinese are a very superstitious people, and such a thing would be quite in keeping with this feature of their character. Of course, the general falling-off is to be accounted for in the usual way; probably some had left because from the very beginning they had neither part nor lot in the matter; while the bulk of them had simply become careless when deprived of the oversight and example of our two brethren.

Before leaving, I visited a number of outside villages with the native preacher, including one about a mile off where several members live, and a few former friends who have gone back again to heathenism. A few of this latter class received me in a kindly way, acknowledging the doctrine to be good, their own intention to resume attendance at Tek-a-kha, and adding with a sigh, 'Ah, how this world does involve us!' Some said they were very poor, and could not afford to lose the time required for worshipping God; and one old brother frankly said that he was a bad man and unworthy to come. Of course, we everywhere did our best to answer objections, explain difficulties, and repeat the invitation of our long-suffering and gracious Master. Yes, blessed be God! 'Yet there is room' for you, and for *you*, and for YOU, too, my poor ignorant sinning brother. We went to another village much further off, where one of the Tek-a-kha members has long been trying to originate a Church movement. I am sorry to say that his efforts do not commend themselves to us. He is plainly an unsafe man; said to have a good deal of questionable business on hand, and will probably have to be suspended from the Communion before long.

I had very mingled feelings during my two days' return journey to the city. I had seen multitudes perishing for lack of knowledge, and our insufficiently cared-for little congregations scattered abroad as sheep having no shepherd. Lord, come to our help and send forth labourers into Thy harvest!

21. *The Canadian Mission.*

KELUNG HARBOUR, 25 *October* 1878.
—I have just had an opportunity of going over a good part of the mission field occupied by the Presbyterian Church of Canada ; but before referring to work carried on there, it may be well to state a few things about our own Po-sia stations which I visited on the way up.

It was on 3d September that the junior colporteur and myself set out from Tai-wanfoo. We passed the first night with our brethren at Hoan-a-chhan, and halted for lunch the following day with a member of our Ka-poa-soa congregation. He told me that since the burning of the chapel in his village, the enemies of the church had been much quieter. They evidently saw that the authorities were compelled to use a firm hand in dealing with those anti-

Christian outrages, while the indemnifying proceeds of erecting a new chapel at the public expense assured them that their day of reckoning had come. It would certainly take a long time to speak of all the persecution we have witnessed in this region during the past few years.

On arriving at Ka-gi city, the County Magistrate paid me an official visit, during which I expressed to him our satisfaction that the decision of the recent Court of Inquiry was being faithfully carried out. This Court was held lately at Giam-cheng under the presidency of two officers of superior rank, and for the express purpose of dealing with the Peh-tsui-khe troubles of 1875, the murder of Un Ong, the chapel-burning at Ka-poa-soa, and many other acts of assault and plunder against our native brethren. It took place in one of the temples, and was rather a grand affair. About two hundred armed soldiers were present, and a part of the proceedings consisted in ten men accompanying the second Commissioner to have the mouldering remains of Ong's body taken up for examination. This item of our complaint was altogether new to those high-class mandarins, as the local Tsong-ia had failed to report the matter. At the close of a very long examination of witnesses, and on my stating that several well-known persecutors were still boasting of what they would do, the second Commissioner replied at once by saying that their heads would be sent down to Taiwanfoo to-morrow! It was ultimately agreed that all the ringleaders should be seized for punishment, that the Tsong-ia and Goa-ui of the district be degraded from office, that the authorities would have a new chapel erected at Ka-poa-soa, and that suitable proclamations would be posted up over all the country. I need only add that the services of Consul Frater have been simply invaluable at this time. Under God, it is to his firm and considerate action that a brighter day has now commenced to shine for us in Ka-gi.

On Thursday our party halted at several large towns, where crowds of people were addressed and some hundreds of tracts were readily purchased. Tau-lak is the name of one of those towns. It lies about thirteen miles to the north-east of Ka-gi and would make a very good stage on our journey to Po-sia, being, moreover, a place where we have always been able to reckon on having crowds of attentive hearers. We spent that evening in the village of Liu-liu-pan. There was no inn here, but the village Elder kindly accommodated us in the back room of a neighbouring little temple. After supper, the people gathered into the open porch in front, to whom we preached and sold leaflets till nearly midnight.

It was on the following day we passed through the market-town of Lim-ki-po, where several dollars'-worth of books and tracts could easily have been sold had it been possible to halt for an hour or so. We met with unusually heavy rains during the afternoon of that day, and the crossing of a number of mountain torrents also helped to retard our progress. Darkness found us wandering about in the bed of one, at a place where bands of head-hunting savages occasionally make their appearance.

The right path had somehow escaped us, and the people were all in bed when we came straggling into the little hamlet of Tsui-li-khe.

Po-sia was reached late on the evening

of the following day, still in the midst of heavy rain; and this, with the dampness of the room in which we took up our quarters, brought on cold and a sharp attack of aguish fever which kept me rather weak for several days. The three Po-sia churches still show signs of spiritual life and progress. It was my privilege to examine over thirty candidates for baptism, and twelve of these were gladly welcomed to the table of the Lord. Arrangements are now in progress for building a new chapel at O-gu-lan, it being decided to use the present chapel for carrying on the successful school-work at this station. One source of much annoyance to the Po-sia people at present is the hostility of the neighbouring savages, who keep lurking about the base of the hills, and rush out whenever the opportunity of obtaining a head presents itself. One of our members was very recently cut off in this way, and the people dare not move about without carrying their weapons with them.

I think it very probable that, before long, very important changes may take place in Po-sia. The Chinese still continue to increase in number, the walls of a new city are now being built, and our Sek-hoan brethren are sure to find it difficult to hold their own under the new order of things. It is, however, very pleasing to know that the entire number of Christian worshippers here must reach about a thousand, and that one often hears of their good conduct, even from those who have no thought of abandoning their idols. There has been an addition of several families to two of the congregations, and only one person had to be excluded from the Communion at this time.

I cannot but refer to the satisfaction with which our brethren and sisters still refer to the late visit of Mr. and Mrs. Ritchie to Po-sia. It was the first occasion on which a European lady had travelled so far north. Her short stay at each of these distant churches has given a decided impulse to the educational work among the female portion of our people, and friends at home are little aware how much we are indebted to Mrs. Ritchie's unfailing cheerfulness, good sense, and activity in helping on the cause of Christ in Formosa.

I remained two Sabbaths in Po-sia, and started for Toa-sia on Thursday, 19th September, arriving there on Saturday the 21st. Three adults were baptized at this station, and the Communion was dispensed on Sabbath the 29th. During the intervening days, several short tours were made to the neighbouring towns, the more important of those visited being Gaw-chay, Goo-ma-thau, Haw-law-tun, and Tang-si-kak, in each of which open-air meetings were held and tracts sold. With a few of the brethren, a visit was also paid to Lai-sia; where great changes have taken place since the time of my last visit. I would be almost afraid to say how many of our brethren and other natives in this valley have recently been murdered by savages. Indeed, the position has become so dangerous that they have determined to abandon the place, and our friends are now engaged in removing their goods and furniture to Toa-sia, only the able-bodied men remaining to act as soldiers till the present crop of rice be gathered in. The savages are quite aware of the intention to come out, and our daily fear is that some general massacre may take place before harvest-time. During my stay at this time, it was almost impossible to sleep at nights for the continual beating of the watch-signals. Three persons were murdered a few weeks before my arrival, and one was beheaded near the village only a few days after I left.

Having thus gone the round of those Chiang-hoa stations, I continued my journey northward to Tamsui, which was reached on the afternoon of the fourth day from Lai-sia. Of course Brother Mackay gave me a right hearty welcome, and accompanied me on a tour of inspection through all his churches.

We have just returned from a six-days' trip over what is called the Kabalan, Kap-tsu-lan, or Gi-lan Plain, on the north-east coast. Our route lay along the seashore as far as Saw Bay, and then by way of Sa-kiet-a-koe, a large town some miles

The Canadian Mission. 527

inland, where Mr. Mackay did a little teeth extracting and the people were spoken to about worshipping the true God.

At Saw Bay I obtained permission to go a day's journey further south in a government junk, but the officials became suspicious as the captain and myself were going on board and prevented me from leaving. The savage territory south of Saw Bay is at present in a very disturbed condition; but, from the place to which the junk was going, a comparatively safe road is said to run across the mountains as far as Heng-chhun, and from that on to Taiwanfoo. I was rather disappointed at meeting with this hindrance, although all that could be done was to table my passport and say to those underlings that they had better be careful what they were about. Here, also, we spent two nights in a large damp temple, where Mr. Mackay had some interesting conversation with the resident priest, who was sick, and evidently in a dying state.

At another village where we passed the night a theatrical company had erected in front of one of the temples; a large covered stage, upon which Mr. Mackay and myself took up our stand before the evening performance commenced and preached to a crowd of about five hundred persons. The scene was a very characteristic one. Two great oil-lamps had been fastened outside, the curious but perfectly well-pleased crowd was immediately in front of us; and further on, the open temple, also lighted up, was filled with its usual collection of gilt idols, burning tapers, smoking incense, and little groups of devout worshippers, from the heathen point of view. We alternately preached there till nearly midnight.

On the following day, an opportunity was given us of seeing a little of the Pi-po-hoan in this part of the island. The bulk of those we met spoke their own language, and very little Chinese; seemed exceedingly poor, and of much less intellectual stamina than their fellow-aborigines of the south. In one village south of Saw Bay, the women who came to see us appeared to have no feeling of delicacy at the decided scantiness of their dress, while the expression on most of the male faces was strongly suggestive of blank ignorance and of cowering timidity. They did not seem to have a single thought about a Creator, and told us that their conformity to Chinese doctrines and practices dated back for only fifty or sixty years. We addressed them for a short time on Gospel subjects, our Toa-sia elder, A-chiang, with one of Mr. Mackay's Pi-po-hoan preachers, also speaking to them of salvation through Christ.

There seemed to be a fine opening all along the plain for the Tamsui Church to go in and possess the land. Mr. Mackay was received as an old friend in some places, although only one or two previous visits had been made. There are at least four large towns here, in any of which, if at home, one would be sure to find several congregations of the Episcopalians, Presbyterians, Congregationalists, Methodists, and Free-thinkers, with all sorts of Missions and Societies for the benefit of saints and sinners alike.

As to that part of the Tamsui field where work is now going on, I have already seen ten of the churches, and my intention is to start from Kelung on Monday first to visit the remaining five. In addition to those fifteen chapels there

The Canadian Mission. 531

are six or seven schools in operation, two Bible-women at work, and six students in daily attendance on Mr. Mackay's instructions. I am told that the entire adult membership is at present a little over two hundred; the two finely-situated bungalows, with a large hospital about to be erected at the Port, also showing the prosperity of our sister mission in Formosa. And yet, it is not from any such bare enumeration that one can know how much has really been accomplished during the past seven years. One requires to see the chapels, to have some acquaintance with those fifteen preachers, and to mingle a little among the members and the much larger body of adherents, in order to judge correctly of a work, not less remarkable in extent than it is singularly healthy and well-developed in all its parts.

There can be no doubt that, so far as the

field itself is concerned, the lines have fallen in pleasant places to the Canadian Mission. A few hours' sail in one of the river boats brings one to the greater number of the out-stations, the scenery in every direction is really grand, the climate colder than at Taiwanfoo, and extreme poverty and ignorance among the people less frequently to be met with than in other parts of the island.

With all this, however, it is necessary to get introduced to God's main instrument in accomplishing the results above referred to. Mr. Mackay is a little man, firm and active, of few words, unflinching courage, and one whose sound common-sense is equalled only by his earnest devotion to the Master. He began by labouring hard to know the language well himself, and came soon to think that, so far as he dared give it direction, his work had better

The Canadian Mission. 533

for a time be confined to the largely predominating Chinese portion of the people. During the first year of his stay in Tamsui, he began an educational and evangelistic training movement among the young men of the Church, which has been greatly blessed in the carrying on of the work. For the most part, the Tamsui chapels are well grouped together, our brother going on the plan of very gradual extension, with occasional long evangelistic tours into regions which are still unoccupied. On such journeys, his real work has been greatly helped by sometimes practising as a dentist in the towns and villages through which he passed. From the chewing of betel-nut and other similar habits, the Chinese suffer much from decaying teeth, so that Mr. Mackay is enabled on a short passing visit to do the maximum of good to the bodies of the people, with a minimum amount of entanglement in mere extraneous matters.

I noticed, too, that great attention has been paid to the praise part of worship in the Tamsui Church. The singing among the brethren is distinct, hearty, and frequent, while our brother himself generally begins any open-air service by singing one of our appropriate Chinese hymns.

22. *In Memoriam.*

LIVERPOOL, 14 *October* 1879.—It is while on furlough here, and engaged in deputation work, that I have just received intelligence of the death of my esteemed colleague Mr. Ritchie. The sad news has been sent by telegraph, so that all we know yet is that fever closed his earthly career at Taiwanfoo on the 29th of last month. The loss to the Mission in For-

REV. HUGH RITCHIE.

In Memoriam.

mosa is very serious, as it is the second such removal from our little company within the present year, dear old Elder Bun having died at Chang-chiu shortly after I visited him there when on the way home.

My acquaintance with Mr. Ritchie dates much further back than that day in 1871 on which he gave me a hearty welcome to Formosa. We came to know a little of each other during our college days in Glasgow about sixteen years ago. He was then a most diligent student and conscientious in the performance of all his duties. His class-fellows were quite aware that he was preparing for future work among the heathen, and it was the fact of everything about the man being so much in keeping with this purpose that led them to entertain for him a feeling of the very highest respect. We liked his frank open way, and one could not be long in his company without seeing that he had a high ideal before him, and meant to live up to it. After spending three sessions at Glasgow, he became a student of the English Presbyterian College in London, and on completing the divinity course there, his long-cherished desire to enter the foreign mission field was realised on receiving an appointment to Formosa.

Of course, I have had the fullest opportunity for getting to know him during the past seven years. He was a most generous friend, a warm-hearted follower of Christ, and an earnest, self-denying, and successful missionary. It was his delight to mingle much prayer with his work, and he was just as mindful of this when thanksgiving had to be offered, as in times of difficulty and trial. I well remember one little incident which showed this characteristic of the man. We had been long toiling up the side of a high mountain, and reached the summit to be rewarded with a cool breeze and a grand view of the country eastward from Taiwanfoo. After resting, Mr. Ritchie proposed to have a little prayer, and we retired to some rocks, where he poured out his soul for the land of our adoption in such a way, that one rose with a much better conception of the duty and the glorious privilege of being a missionary amongst the heathen. His death must be sorely felt by the native brethren in Formosa, for they never had a more kind and sympathising friend. He was always planning something for their benefit, and nothing gave him more delight than to see them growing in grace and in the knowledge of our Lord and Saviour Jesus Christ. Well did he know that there was no other way to a, happy and useful life, and his own fine bracing example supplied the most convincing proof of this. The work he was enabled to do in Formosa will continue for many years to bear fruit to the glory of God. May other like-minded labourers be speedily raised up! At no previous time in the history of the Mission has there been a better opportunity for work, and the thought is rather a depressing one that so little is being done to fill up the sadly-thinning number of those engaged in it.

With regard to the memory of dear old Bun also, I cannot but cherish the tenderest and most grateful feelings. He was truly a spiritual father to me during my first three years' work in Formosa, but I shall content myself here by simply quoting Dr. Maxwell's words regarding him:—

'Our departed brother and elder in the

In Memoriam. 539

Church was a signal witness to what the grace of Christ can do in and by a Chinaman. Bun was not a man of superior "gifts," and his education had been very meagre. For many years he had been an opium-smoker, and his employment as a tax-gatherer was not one in which the better qualities of Chinese human nature find much stimulus to development.

'But on the other hand was the fact that at his conversion he had accepted Christ with his *whole* heart. The Master drew all that was in the man into His own service, and gave the new weapon an edge which increased in keenness with daily use. If other gifts were only common, there was at least a *rare spiritual* gift. His whole heart was in his Master's work, and constantly on the alert.

'He accompanied the first foreign missionary to Formosa to occupy, as was supposed, the humble office of chapel-keeper; but he speedily became the missionary's right hand in the work. He was ever ready to speak for Christ—in the Chapel, on the streets, in the hospital, in itinerant tours, but most of all to individuals; and this diligence in work for others was fitly matched by his unfailing delight in the personal use of the Word, and in secret prayer. His advanced years, even when he first reached Formosa, and the entire absence from his Christian character of anything like trifling, made his presence in the mission of great value. Not only the members and adherents of the Church, but the outside heathen learned to respect the Christian dignity of the old elder. He became the constant referee in all matters of difficulty which arose amongst the native brethren. And other curious matters would occasionally come

ELDER BUN.

In Memoriam. 541

before him. Sometimes the missionary and his wife have welcomed the old man, when he would unexpectedly come in upon them at a meal-time, to find that his object was to have a little quiet talk with them about some servant whose ideas of rule and order were a little less strict than theirs, and who had carried his grievances to the worthy elder. He himself was very forbearing and gentle. Only once in the course of six years' constant intercourse did the writer see Bun thoroughly vexed and angry. Our brother was earnestly addressing an audience in the Taiwanfoo chapel when a man quietly leant over the table and gave him a violent blow in the chest. The mean way in which the blow was dealt nettled the old man, and some of the friendly bystanders having seized the offender, he was held in rather a firm grasp till the missionary was sent for. On

Bun himself being quietly appealed to, however, as to what course was most likely to advantage the Lord's cause, he at once calmed down and willingly consented that with a word of caution the man should be dismissed. The man had meanwhile become rather ashamed of his conduct, and promised not to repeat it.

'When he left Formosa, the well-thumbed Testament which he had so often used in chapel was given to Mr. Campbell as a parting remembrance. It is before me as I write, and I see that underneath Mr Campbell's name he has indicated two texts, 2 Cor. i. 8-11, and 2 Cor. xii. 9. If the reader will take the trouble to consult them, and call to mind the very marvellous deliverance from "so great a death" and "in Asia" which Mr. Campbell had just experienced, he will realise the aptness of the old elder's choice of the first text, and the preciousness also of its union with the second.

'There are many in Formosa, and two or three in England, to whom the remembrance of Elder Bun will ever be as a sweet savour of Christ, and there are not a few—some already gone up higher, and more still living—who will be his " crown of rejoicing in the presence of our Lord Jesus Christ at His coming."'

23. *A Christian Conference.*

TAIWANFOO, 12 *January* 1883.—The Mission in Formosa has not yet committed itself to any elaborate system of church government. When a score or two of converts have been gathered together in any place, we have never delayed long in advising them to choose out several of the more intelligent of their number that they might be set apart to the eldership and deaconship of the congregation; but, beyond the Session meetings held with those brethren on the occasion of our own visits, we can hardly yet be said to have adopted the Presbyterian form of Church order. In place of stated Presbytery meetings, we have held more informal gatherings from time to time, to which all the office-bearers were invited for mutual counsel and earnest waiting upon God.

The first of these general Conferences was held in December 1874, when the elders, deacons, and native preachers connected with the Takow and Taiwanfoo branches of the Mission met with us at the former centre, and greatly benefited by the meetings which were then held. The second Conference took place the following year, when a company of brethren from

A Christian Conference. 545

the Canadian Mission and the office-bearers of the South Formosa churches had several days of profitable fellowship in Taiwanfoo. It was then arranged that the next series of meetings should be held towards the close of 1876 at one of the Tamsui stations. Two of the English Presbyterian missionaries and a large deputation of their native friends attended those meetings at Toalong-pong, and carried away very pleasing recollections of God's goodness to the Church in Formosa, and of the overflowing kindness shown to them by their brethren in the north.

Our fourth Conference took place in Taiwanfoo during the closing days of last month. It had been about seven years since similar meetings were held in the city, and we thought it well that this year the elders, deacons, and preachers should again have the opportunity of coming together for prayer, and praise, and friendly discussion on things concerning the Kingdom. The notices were issued some weeks beforehand, so that every one was sufficiently informed as to the particular business on hand. There was also much prayer on the part of not a few that God would be graciously pleased to use this occasion for reviving His people, and for blessing the whole Church through our meetings.

About one hundred brethren were able to respond to our invitation, for whom suitable arrangements were made during the four days of their stay. We met for the first time on Saturday evening, 24th December. After prayer and some hearty singing, the members listened with much evident sympathy to an address of welcome, which took the form of an exposition of the 122d Psalm. Like the Israelites of

A Christian Conference. 547

old, those native friends had come from all quarters and from distant places to have this happy reunion with each other in the capital city. It was a time of joy, a time for gratitude to their unchanging Lord, and of well-wishing for the peace of Jerusalem.

On the following day three services were held, at the second of which all the Church members present united in that act of remembrance which is the most sacred and endearing to the Christian heart. The chapel was crowded to overflowing. Eight elders assisted, two from each of the four counties now occupied by the Mission. Steadfast little Tiong was one of them, the only survivor of that band of four baptized by Mr. Swanson on 12th August 1866 as the first-fruits of the Church in Formosa, and the same brother who was called on to take up a prominent place of suffering during the persecutions of 1868-9. Before 'the breaking of bread,' those present listened attentively while I spoke of the prophetic and historical references to the mourning of believers in looking on Him whom they have pierced.

Our evening meeting took the form of an open Conference, the greater number of the preachers giving short statements as to the spiritual condition of the churches under their charge. Suitable prayer and praise were mingled with those interesting accounts. The whole day was one to gladden one's heart, a very noticeable thing being the hearty feeling of brotherliness which prevailed among all who were present.

After early morning worship on Monday, the first meeting of the Conference proper took place at ten o'clock, the proceedings continuing till noon, and the subject for consideration being, 'In what condition must the Church be in order to God being well pleased?' After an opening address from the president, the native brethren at once commenced to offer remarks on the subject in an earnest, intelligent, and most orderly way. The two hours seemed to pass long before everything had been said, and all appeared to be benefited and pleased with the meeting.

The subject of the afternoon discussion was, 'In what way can the office-bearers of the Church most efficiently fill their respective duties?' Here, too, the brethren gave evidence of having carefully thought over the matter before rising to speak, and almost every one said something about the need of holy living in private, in the family, in the Church, and in the world, on the part of those who stood forth as officers, so to speak, in the Christian army.

Another suggestive and valuable meeting was that at which a discussion took place on the best means of bringing our Church adults and children to be able to consult the Word of God for themselves. One practical result of this will no doubt be the commencement of systematic Sabbath-school work in Formosa. 'How the heathen could be brought to embrace Christ as their Saviour,' was a question which was also considered by us. On the whole, I believe that much good will flow from those meetings. We know our weak points better now, and our hearts are more cheered to think that much is being done which is fitted to make us steadfast and unmovable, always abounding in the work of the Lord.

24. Interruption from the French.

AMOY, 24 November 1884.—The present Franco-Chinese trouble has now come very near to us, and the following statement gives only a brief outline of what has been taking place during the past few weeks.

It was early in September that the people of Taiwanfoo were startled to learn that the northern Port of Ke-lung had been bombarded, and that French men-of-war might be hourly expected to commence hostilities in the south of the island. As the missionaries are the only European residents in the capital, our position soon came to be somewhat uncomfortable, if not even a little dangerous. The unsettling rumours which got into circulation had plainly some foundation of truth in them, and if they had been followed up by the threatened outbreak of rowdyism and anti-foreign excitement, it was easy to see that, humanly speaking, our escape would have been almost impossible. In such a case the privilege of British nationality would have been no protection to us whatever, the Chinese being quite unable to distinguish one 'outer barbarian' from another, even although they wished to do so. I still remember the mistakes which were constantly being made when the Japanese landed an armed force in South Formosa ten years ago. It was then a thing of daily occurrence for intelligent Chinamen to ask if we and the Japanese inhabited the same country, spoke the same language, and were all subject to the same *Hoan-ong*, or foreign king? And so at the present time. With the great mass of the people, the strong feeling and opposition being shown is far less anti-French than it is anti-foreign.

About the middle of September, matters became so critical in Taiwanfoo that the authorities interdicted us from continuing the visitation of our country stations, while soon after we were unanimous in thinking that, for a time at least, our students ought to be dismissed to their homes. I may add that, for weeks before, hundreds of well-to-do people had been removing their families to places of safety in the low-lying hill-region eastward from Taiwanfoo. Our work was thus brought virtually to a stand-still, and it was during that interval of prayerful, anxious waiting that we received an official circular from Takow—about thirty miles distant—which seemed to call for still more decided action upon our part. This circular was sent to us by the commander of a British gunboat stationed at Takow, and began by stating that, from information received, an early bombardment of the southern Ports might be looked for, but that protection would be afforded to Europeans by coming on board within one hour after notice had been given by the sounding of an alarm bell. The circular went on to say that, when the Takow people were all on board, the gunboat would immediately steam up to An-peng to give similar opportunity to any residents there who wished to avail themselves of the protection of the British flag. The position of our mission party in these circumstances will be better understood if I add that Taiwanfoo is situated fully three miles inland from the port at An-peng, while vessels anchoring require to lie in the open roadstead about two miles off from the shore.

In keeping, therefore, with the informa-

Interruption from the French. 555

tion which was conveyed by this circular, and acting on the advice of the Consul, we at once arranged for having the ladies brought over to Amoy; it being also decided that only as many of the missionaries should remain in Taiwanfoo as would secure a continuance of the work carried on in the hospital. I brought over the archives of the Mission with those who came to the mainland; but, a few days after our arrival, tidings came of the bombardment of Tamsui, with an official notice that the French had placed the whole western side of the island under what was called 'a pacific but strict blockade.' Dr. Anderson and Mr. Thow have thus been shut up in Taiwanfoo for the last six weeks. We have been repeatedly refused the opportunity of relieving them, and communication with Formosa has been entirely cut off.

About a month ago, Dr. Mackay, of the Canadian Mission, passed through Amoy on his way to join his family at Hong-Kong. He then supplied us with a very graphic and a very sad account of what had recently taken place in the northern part of the Island. It was estimated that the French must have poured upwards of a thousand shells into Tam-sui alone. Their firing was criticised as having been of the most wild and reckless nature. Every European house was struck, and nearly every member of the small foreign community was exposed for whole days to the most alarming and imminent danger. A piece of a shell, weighing upwards of thirty pounds, smashed through the roof of Dr. Mackay's house, and buried itself in the floor of the hall, at a place where people were constantly passing. Dr. Mackay also stated that a wide-spread and

Interruption from the French. 557

serious outbreak had taken place against the native Christians. . Two of them had been speared to death by Chinese rowdies, and no fewer than seven of those fine northern chapels had been levelled to their foundations. May God send speedy deliverance to His people! We rejoice to learn that, till five weeks ago, our brethren in the south have been preserved from such painful and bitter experiences.

Of course, it is impossible to say when we may return to Formosa, or what may be the conditions under which our work will be resumed. The general opinion here is that severe fighting must take place both in north and south Formosa before very long, and that, in view of this, all the foreigners who are there at present will receive an official notice to quit the Island. One thing we earnestly desire is that, when we do return, it may not be to find hundreds of Frenchmen in permanent or temporary possession of the place.

To refer now to Amoy. Nothing could exceed the kindness of our missionary friends here when, somewhat empty-handed, we arrived among them fully two months ago. Dr. Maxwell did not come over with the first party, and a good deal of sickness prevailed among us for more than a fortnight after our arrival; but no one could have done more for us than Dr. MacLeish, and his self-denying kindness is something which will not be easily forgotten by us.

Another item which presented to us the bright side of things was the fact that, in coming to Amoy, we came to mingle with native brethren who speak the same dialect as our own people in Formosa; at a time, too, when it grieves one to see this oldest centre of our Mission with only four colleagues to undertake an amount of work which might well tax the energies of ten. For my own part, it has been a great joy and privilege to visit such places as Pechuia and An-hai, and to see these fully-organised congregations having their own native pastors and teachers, and carrying on a work which is bringing light and gladness to many a poor heathen heart.

My late two weeks' sojourn in the Chinchew and Eng-chhun prefectures was truly a time of great privilege. The last time I travelled over this road was with Dr. Douglas in 1874. Every one knows that it was a favourite journey with him. Ah! yes, how he prayed and toiled and waited for the coming of Christ's kingdom in this region, and how it would have rejoiced his heart to see the way in which it is now opening up to the gracious and healing influence of the Gospel! What a grand old city is Chin-chew! In our field there is nothing at all to compare with it; its ancient history, literary renown, and large population being far ahead of anything to be seen in Formosa. Dr. Grant, of the Amoy Mission, has his hospital here, and he is the only European resident in the city. I have never met with any man who seems more thoroughly beloved by people both inside of the Church and out of it. His abundant labours in the hospital are fast opening up a large and most magnificent region inland from Chin-chew, about which our mainland brethren will have something interesting to say before very long. I was myself charmed with the country all along the north bank of the river, while the Eng-chhun valley appeared to me to be simply an ideal spot in which an inland branch of the Mission

Interruption from the French. 561

might be established at some future time. The old Elder who accompanied me knew the region well, and led on through the Prefectural city to a number of large villages, where the people most gladly listened to all that was said to them.

On the return journey, we halted for a night in the house of Brother Kiet, who attends the services at Sian-oan. I was greatly pleased with this man. He accompanied me to the chapel on Saturday, and it was my privilege to receive him and another man into Church membership on the following day. In various out-of-the-way places we met with persons who had been inmates of the hospital at Chinchew; and the roll of patients there shows that thousands of such people must be scattered throughout this part of the country. What a pity that two or three mission families cannot now be spared to go and take up their residence in Chinchew! Why don't the Church at home send out a like-minded clerical brother to labour with Dr. Grant?

25. *Happy Days at Amoy.*

AMOY, 13 *April* 1885.—The French blockade still continues, and there is no getting over to Formosa. It is a great comfort that, during this season of exile, we do not require to remain in enforced idleness. Our Amoy brethren give us every facility for being useful, and the Island-missionaries have no linguistic difficulty in speaking with the Chinese of this region. As work among them is quite identical with our own, some notes of a recent journey may appropriately be inserted here.

I left Amoy on the 14th of last month,

Happy Days at Amoy.

and reached Pechuia about noon the same day. It is usual for the missionaries to halt at Pechuia on their way to other stations, in order to confer with Pastor Tan Leng about little matters which are always arising at one or other of the country churches. I spent some two hours with him on this occasion, and could not but feel what a very helpful man our Amoy brethren have in this worthy Chinese co-presbyter.

Going on afterwards to Iu-boe-kio, I arrived at the chapel there a little before sunset. Tek-tsu is the preacher now stationed at Iu-boe-kio. He is one of the older servants of the Mission; and while sitting late with him that evening after worship, I listened with much interest to the useful information he gave me about the early history of the little congregations in this neighbourhood. Tek-tsu himself is a fine sort of man; active, well-informed, and with, I should say, a good deal of quiet enduring earnestness about him. It is quite evident he has been deeply impressed with the example of the late W. C. Burns, and it was very refreshing to listen to his reminiscences of that devoted servant of God.

On Sabbath the 15th I was up betimes, and after prayer with a few friends who came in, started for the village of Aw-sai, to enter the chapel in that place just as the brethren had concluded forenoon worship. At the afternoon service I addressed an attentive audience on Paul's statement about having learned, in whatsoever state he was, to be content. We had a smaller meeting in the evening, when a further opportunity was given me of exhorting the brethren to adorn the doctrine of God our Saviour in all things.

It may be well to mention here that the congregations at Iu-boe-kio, Aw-sai, and Liong-bun-si are united under one Session, the sacraments being dispensed once a quarter at each place in rotation. The brethren were now looking forward to have their next general meeting at Liong-bun-si, on Sabbath first; and, as I had engaged to undertake whatever pastoral work might then be necessary, there were several spare days for visiting the Church members, or evangelising throughout the region.

On Monday the 16th, I was much pleased to find that two colporteurs and three of the preachers had arrived to join me in this much-needed work of preaching among the country villages. We had an early meeting for prayer and a short consideration of Christ's charge to His twelve disciples, and then left for a village about two miles distant, in good hope that favourable opportunities for speaking would be granted us, and that God would use our message for stirring the hearts of those who are perishing for lack of knowledge. On entering, we found that many of the people were out at work in their fields, but we no sooner went to the village temple, than the building became filled with women and children, and about a score of elderly men. I began by saying we had come to them with good news that morning, even to tell them how they could all be made holy and happy, both for time and eternity. The first twelve verses of St. Matthew's Gospel were then read, and a long address followed on the way by which *they* could attain to the character and blessedness of the man therein described. It was very encouraging to observe the respectful attention paid by the female portion of the

Happy Days at Amoy. 567

audience ; one old woman, in particular, giving earnest heed to the things which were spoken, and at the close asking me if all I had been saying were really true. Several short addresses from the others were afterwards given ; and before leaving, the people purchased from us over two hundred *cash*-worth of Christian tracts.

We then removed to a village about three miles off in another direction, one object of our going there being to have some conversation with a Church member who required to be spoken to about his long-continued absence from public worship. I was glad this brother took in very good part all we said to him. He did not attempt to justify himself, but frankly acknowledged that he had been living in a careless way for years past ; that, during all this time, he had been very unhappy ; but that, with God's help, he would again begin to try and walk worthy of the vocation wherewith he was called.

After this, more than an hour was spent by us in addressing a crowd of the villagers who assembled at the foot of a large tree, and who listened to our message with much apparent intelligence and goodwill. One man asked what kind of ceremonies were to be used in the worship of God—if it was necessary to burn incense-sticks or gilt paper in presenting any petition to Him. Of course, the Chinese know nothing whatever of worship in the Christian sense of the word, and it is almost impossible to get them to understand what is meant by adoration, or praise, or spiritual communion with God. They offer brief petitions to their idols only when threatened with present evil, or in order to obtain some mere worldly good; so that the sight of a Christian company engaged

Happy Days at Amoy.

in lengthened prayer or praise to vacancy —as it seems—is always a puzzle to the heathen mind. I remember the Sek-hoan of Lai-sia telling me, years ago, that when Dr. Maxwell paid his first visit to them, great doubts were entertained when they were asked to close their eyes while trying to join in with the prayers that were offered. The worthy Doctor probably little thought that, for some days during the commencement of Christian work there, a number of those hardy mountaineers kept their weapons at hand, and took their turn at watching him through their open fingers during prayer, in case any injury might have been done to them.

On the way back to Aw-sai for some refreshment, we halted at a third village, and it was here that Colporteur Ham agreeably surprised me by giving a most thoughtful, interesting, and spirited address.

The people were immensely pleased with his rather humorous way of putting some things, and appeared to be just as much impressed when he spoke to them of their sinfulness, and of the salvation provided for them in Christ Jesus. Poor Ham is one of the three brethren who lately received three hundred blows before the District Magistrate for helping to secure chapel premises in the neighbouring city of Chang-poo. I put him down as being rather dull and somewhat listless in his work, but had now received a lesson on the mistake of making up one's mind too hastily, and of judging from a regard to mere outward appearances. While trudging along towards Aw-sai that afternoon, Ham seemed to be much pleased with the few encouraging remarks I made about his really good address.

The latter part of the afternoon was

occupied in visiting a number of brethren who are under Church discipline for neglect of ordinances ; some of them for conduct even much more unbecoming. It should be remembered that such lapsed members are exposed to very much temptation, the wonder being that their spiritual life should hold out longer than a day amid the influences which surround them. One thing is certain, that when they do begin to absent themselves from public worship, their downward course is oftentimes but a mere question of time. Few of them are able to read the Scriptures for themselves, by far the greater number being dependent on the preacher for their knowledge of Christian truth. It is thus very evident that, besides faithfulness, one requires to have a very tender, loving heart in dealing with such brethren ; and O the need of God's own Spirit of grace to impart life, and bring back those poor wanderers to the love and service of the Lord!

The whole of Tuesday the 17th was spent by us in itinerating among a number of villages to the north-west of Aw-sai. We returned in the evening with hoarse voices and tired limbs, but feeling glad and grateful that the Lord had opened for us so large a door of entrance. The people everywhere were most friendly, and seemed to think themselves highly honoured in being visited by a deputation consisting of one foreigner and five well-dressed natives. At nearly every halting-place they brought out chairs and forms for our accommodation; and in one village the kindly, simple-hearted people had a table placed outside, on which were provided for us little dishes containing tea, and the choicest collection of Chinese sweetmeats that could be had. I suppose that our audience in the village of White-Leaf Grove must have numbered about two hundred. They seemed very much interested in every one of the short addresses which were given; and, at the close, purchased from us between two and three hundred *cash*-worth of tracts.

Wednesday the 18th was a day of pouring, continuous rain, and early that morning I told my hearty little company of workers to begin their preparations at once, as I intended to examine them in the evening on everything they could find out about St. Paul's Epistle to Titus. The examination was to be *vivâ voce*, and in order to economise time, all the questions put to them would be written out. I have seldom seen so much diligence shown in preparing for any examination. In order to lay a good foundation, and in the hope that nothing would escape them, the colporteurs made the most strenuous efforts to commit the whole Epistle to memory; while the preachers, fearing lest the attack might come upon them from another direction, dived into the meaning of the Chinese characters, made out all sorts of indexes, and ransacked the Acts and the other Epistles for notices of Titus and the island of Crete. We had evening worship at seven o'clock, and then retired to an upper room of the chapel, where two hours and a half were spent in examining, and in giving them as complete and accurate a view of the contents of the Epistle as I was able. Their answers came quite up to my expectation, and I can truly say that every one of us felt benefited by this effort to know more of Titus, and of his interesting and important work.

The morning of Thursday the 19th

found us all similarly occupied with the Sermon on the Mount; but about ten o'clock the rain ceased and the sky brightened up with the promise of a beautiful afternoon and evening. We accordingly called a halt to our studies, and were soon after on the way for a group of villages which had not yet been visited by any of the preachers. On nearing the first one, we could not explain the presence of an unusual number of men, but learned that, when driven from their work by the rain, they had betaken themselves to gambling in several large empty barns, and were by no means disposed to hasten to their fields when an opportunity was given them for doing so. They listened to us for a short time, but it was evident that the gambling had much more attraction for them than the doctrine. I fear we did little good in that village. Nor had we much success at our next halting-place, the interruption this time coming from scores of mischievous boys, who kept up so much shouting and skylarking among themselves, that it was impossible to obtain a patient hearing. The barking of several coarse, wolfish-looking dogs which persisted in following us, also contributed to our annoyance and disgust. A much better reception awaited us at the following stage, where about a hundred of the villagers came out and quietly listened to us. The majority of them were women, a class it is almost impossible to reach, except by evangelising in this way, or speaking to them in their own homes. The absurd practice of foot-binding is one of the devil's own devices for preventing the women of China from walking any little distance to attend our chapels.

It was with some regret that, after

prayer on the morning of Friday the 20th, we all prepared to separate, the preachers to be in time for their preparatory work on Saturday, the colporteurs to the south, and myself for a Session meeting in view of the Communion services at Liong-bun-si on Sabbath first. I spent the whole of the following week with several brethren in this preaching and visiting work among the villages of the Khi-boe region, and reached Amoy just in time for the meetings of Presbytery which were held on the opening days of this month.

I returned with a deep conviction that our present position in China very much requires that we should aim at some such combination of pastoral, evangelistic, and teaching work as has now been indicated. Many of our preachers have to be sent out after a most imperfect course of training. They are stationed in villages where they meet with little sympathy from their neighbours, sometimes not even from those who ought to be their warmest friends. What I feel therefore is that, more and more, we should aim at being away from our centres for months at a time, at gathering together five or six of the preachers of some district, and at conducting with them special courses of teaching and preaching. The work carried on in our Theological and Middle schools is certainly of great importance, and we require a great deal more of it; but the branch of which I am now speaking is that which must have gone on among the Galilean hills, and as the little company came down south, or extended their journeyings beyond the Jordan. Nothing, too, like united work of this kind for developing the latent energies of the missionary himself. In the Seminary or School, unquestioning obedience is the order of the day; but once let a man take the road with five or six sharp, earnest young fellows, and he must be either an angel or an ass who will not require his whole wits about him.

From the present experience, there is at least *one individual* who would do well to attend to the following: *First*, The need of more careful preparation for a journey like this—preparation for work among the Church members, for class-work with the preachers, and especially for going out to speak to those still sitting in the region and shadow of death. *Second*, The need for giving much greater prominence to the written Word—less answering of heathen objections, of moral discourse, and even of mere expounding; and more, much more, prayerful selection of, and clear distinct reading of, God's own message to sinful men.

After the Blockade.

TAIWANFOO, 30*th* May 1886.— The French blockade of Formosa is now a thing of the past, and we are here at work again as if nothing had happened. It lasted from 20th October till 15th April, and proved a very testing-time to many of the native Christians. The Chinese think of the Church so much as a mere foreign institution, and they have such difficulty in distinguishing among the 'barbarians' of other lands, that one can easily see how an event like this should stir the popular mind, and expose our converts to the suspicion and enmity of those around them.

It is, however, a matter for profound thankfulness that no anti-Christian outbreak has taken place at any of our stations. Rumours did frequently get into circulation that an evil day was awaiting our native brethren for their supposed disloyalty in coming under the influence of foreigners, but month after month passed, and now we are able to say that the record contains not a single instance of open suffering for righteousness' sake. There can be no doubt that the authorities were very vigilant in the preservation of public order, and that much was due to their notifications informing the people about all missionaries here belonging to a nation which had now most friendly relations with the Government at Peking.

In this respect our brethren of the northern Canadian Mission passed through a very different experience; but even there, it is just possible that the destruction of seven chapels, and repeated attacks on people connected with the Church, arose more from pure rowdyism and love of plunder than from hatred of Christianity, as such. The fact that it was only in this region of Formosa where actual fighting took place between the French and Chinese forces sufficiently accounts for the lawlessness which prevailed. All civil administration in Tamsui was suspended for a time, and the military authorities had their attention too much engrossed with other matters to keep down every little local disturbance among the people. We are glad to learn that there is some likelihood of an indemnity being obtained for all this damage to Mission and private property.

One serious result of the blockade is the interruption it has caused to the prosecution of nearly every branch of our ordinary work. The students have lost about nine months' teaching, and the pas-

After the Blockade. 583

toral work at all the out-stations cannot but be in a very backward condition. It is not here as at our long-established Missions on the mainland, where most efficient native pastors are able to do everything that we can do. We are not far enough advanced to have any native pastors in Formosa, nor can it even be said that those who act as evangelists and preachers have received any large amount of training. Hence the need for our own continual presence among the congregations, and the evils which arise if this important department of duty fails to receive its due amount of attention.

We have seen enough since our return to awaken most grateful feelings in thinking of the steadfastness of our native brethren during this season of trial, and for the loyal way in which the native preachers discharged their duties in our absence. The services at each of the churches in the south were held as usual, the peculiar circumstance of being for months cut off from all communication with the outer world appearing only to bring God's people more closely together, and make them more fervent in prayer for grace and all needed protection.

My own belief is that good to China in the higher sense will come out of this Franco-Chinese trouble. Even already it has diffused a better knowledge of other lands, and therefore helped to break down that conservative and self-sufficient spirit which opposes the advance of Christian truth. We here are now eagerly looking forward to great and speedy advance being made by the churches in Formosa.

27. Other fell on Good Ground.

TAIWANFOO, 7 October 1885.—The following account of a journey from which I returned yesterday may not be without interest.

One of our very promising students named Ang-Khe accompanied me, and we started early on Thursday the 24th *ult.*, our intention being to visit several stations in the county immediately north of the one in which Taiwanfoo is situated. This county of Ka-gi occupies the middle part of the island on its western side, and stated missionary work commenced in it about the beginning of 1872. There was a good deal of opposition at first, but we have now no fewer than six little Christian congregations in the Ka-gi region, while there seems good reason to hope that all this is merely the first-fruits of a much more rapid and even healthier extension of the work.

On the day Ang-Khe and myself set out, several halting-places furnished us with very good opportunities for wayside preaching. This was particularly the case at Hm-kang-boe, as traggling market-town about sixteen miles to the north of Taiwanfoo. We spent more than an hour in front of a shop there which had painted over it the two large characters for 'Complete Happiness.' Friends at home would scarcely think that a descriptive title of this kind would be used over the door of an opium-shop; yet such was the case. The use of the drug has fearfully increased of late years in Formosa, and many of the people have long since given up all feeling of shame in owning their connection with it. They regard opium as being simply indispensable to their daily comfort, while the sale of the article is found to be so profitable that every means is taken to increase the consumption.

We spent the first night at Kiam-tsui-kang, said to be one of the largest towns on the island. It stands about three miles in from the sea and an equal distance from the direct main road to Ka-gi city. The place has bee frequently visited by us, and a good many old hospital patients are to be found in the neighbourhood. The result however is that, so far as we know, Kiam-tsui-kang still remains shrouded in spiritual darkness. After our arrival on this occasion, I preached to a large crowd till the lateness of the hour compelled us to disperse. There was no little interruption from time to time, one or two remarking that we were merely French spies; others, that we were foreigners trying to find new openings for the sale of opium; a few, that we were travelling doctors; but the greater number, that we were good men going about exhorting people to the practice of virtue.

We started again on Friday morning, and after about three hours of tiresome travelling, arrived at the large village of Gu-ta-oan. As we had arranged to spend the night here, and as this name is likely to become a familiar one to our Mission, it may not be out of place to add a few words about the object and result of the present visit. Six months have not yet elapsed since we came first to know that an interest in the Gospel had been awakened in Gu-ta-oan. None of us having ever visited the place, and the name being a new one, it was described to us as a considerable Chinese village some twelve miles to the south-west of the county city in Ka-gi. More definite information was obtained from hree of the students on returning from their summer holidays. They halted for some time at Gu-ta-oan on their way down to Taiwanfoo, and saw enough to convince them that the people sincerely desired to know the truths of the Gospel, about thirty of them having renounced all connection with idolatry, and being daily engaged in the study of the New Testament and hymn-book.

I was thus to some extent prepared for the warm welcome with which many of these villagers received us that evening. They abandoned their fields on our account, provided a suitable lodging for us, brought forth substantial material for our refreshment, and took every way of showing their joy and thankfulness at our presence amongst them. They also conducted me to a neighbouring village, where five or six entire families had ceased the worship of idols, and were now under such Christian instruction as could be obtained. A general meeting was speedily convened of all those who had cast in their lot with us, many outsiders being present, and every one showing an amount of respectful attention that was truly encouraging. The apartment in which we met proving rather confined, a large table was placed on the open ground outside, and, standing upon this, we preached alternately till we were thoroughly tired. More than a hundred people gathered round. It was the time of clear full-moon, and I have seldom spoken under circumstances more stimulating and impressive. After much interesting conversation at the close, one brother offered a site, while about twenty others engaged to put up a suitable place of worship at their own expense. It was agreed that a building with bamboo frame-

Other fell on Good Ground. 591

work would be quite sufficient to meet present requirements.

So far as I could learn, it appears that the beginning of this movement among the people of Gu-ta-oan dates much further back than the present year. They told me that, about three years ago, a number of the villagers were wandering about in search of employment; that two of them found their way to the Christian village of Giam-cheng, where Deacon Tsu-ong met them, treated them with kindness, and, from the very commencement, spoke to them of obtaining salvation through the mercy of God. He also presented a copy of the small hymn-book used at our prayer-meetings to one of these men, who returned soon after to express his warm interest in the invitation to become a worshipper of the true and living God. It was also about this time that a Gu-ta-oan man went to the city of Ka-gi to take up his residence there, and heard from a church adherent something about his need of the salvation provided through Jesus Christ. The Ka-gi elder Se-keng then went down to spend a Sabbath at Gu-ta-oan, and found a little company of brethren awaiting him; who, considering their opportunities, had acquired an amount of Christian knowledge which both surprised and delighted him.

Before I left on Saturday morning, they requested that Ang-khe should be allowed to remain for eight or ten days to see after the building of the chapel, and to have reading-classes with them every evening after worship. I readily assented to this, and parted from them soon after with something of the feelings of a man who had just discovered a silver-mine. I have no doubt that many of the fine promising

Other fell on Good Ground. 593

lads at Gu-ta-oan will yet be able to give a good account of themselves, as several of the grown-up people are already speaking of sending their sons to the Middle School at Taiwanfoo.

One or two things have arrested my attention in connection with this fresh extension of the work :—*First*, the instrumentality which God's Spirit has used for bringing it about has been the Christian character and faithfulness of the native brethren themselves ; *Second*, the value of our simple little hymn-book as a medium for the conveyance of spiritual truth. It is a small collection of only some fifty-nine hymns, yet containing a remarkably full statement of all the leading doctrines of the Bible ; presented too in a form that is not less simple than it is very easily remembered. Might it not be a good thing for brethren at all the churches to spend a part of every Sabbath in finding out passages of Scripture confirmatory of the sentences in our hymn-book. *Third*, another interesting thing I noticed at Gu-ta-oan was the fact already hinted at, namely, that the worshippers there are largely made up of entire families who have—still, doubtless, with much imperfection—declared themselves to be on the Lord's side. I saw old women encouraging their sons, and wives their husbands, to a life of diligent obedience to the truth. We were very sorry to part from each other; and had it not been that arrangements were made for having special services with our brethren in the county city on Sabbath, I should most gladly have remained with them for several days.

Starting therefore on Saturday morning, I was able to reach Ka-gi in good time to examine the candidates for baptism who had been brought forward. Of these, it was decided that two should be received, one of them being that Gu-ta-oan brother who had come to take up his quarters in the city. The Ka-gi office-bearers were able to give me a very favourable report of the continued prosperity of the Church in this important centre. There were no cases of discipline, and the brethren were continuing to show an encouraging amount of sincerity in their Christian profession. The services on Lord's day were well attended, and altogether my visit was a very pleasant and profitable one to myself. For a few days at the beginning of the week, I was occupied in visiting the brethren in their homes, and otherwise trying to make the most of my stay amongst them.

On Thursday, I started for a large market-town called Tau-lak, about a day's journey to the north of Ka-gi city, and lying on the direct route to our stations in the Po-sia region. We had often halted here for preaching in the open marketplace, but with no apparent result till the spring of 1883, when several persons commenced to manifest an interest in the Gospel. Mr. Barclay was privileged to baptize three men from T'au-lak about six months ago. In all, some thirty meet statedly for worship, and there is good reason to hope that here, too, we may have the joy of soon seeing a much-needed and prosperous little church. The whole region is a very populous one, and such a light as this would be sure to bring brightness and joy to many a wretched soul. On the evening of my visit, about forty persons met and listened attentively to an exposition of the miraculous draught of fishes as recorded in St. Luke.

I returned to Ka-gi on Friday afternoon,

and on the following morning started south to be in time for the Communion services at Giam-cheng on 4th *inst*. A part of the preliminary work included the examination of five persons who came forward for baptism. One of them was Chhiah-be, a young man who has been a hearer for some time. He is now acting as schoolmaster at Giam-cheng, and has certainly suffered a great deal on account of—no other apparent reason than—his profession of Christianity. I believe myself that Chhiah-be is sincere in his profession, although unable to see my way to admit him on this occasion. After being under examination for about half an hour, he became strangely excited, and evidently nothing would disabuse his mind of the belief that the Holy Spirit in the form of a bright object was always hovering in front of him. I don't lay a great deal of stress on this. It is quite plain that the poor fellow is in a very feverish, weak condition of body; and what was of far more value from an evidential point of view, was the testimony of the preacher in charge, who had been in close fellowship with him for the past five months, and who was convinced of the sincerity of his desire to be a Christian. I think that upon the next occasion of a pastoral visit, there is every likelihood that Chhiah-be will be received. I baptized two men and one woman at this time, besides setting apart two brethren as Deacons and two to the office of the Eldership. The members at Giam-cheng are a good deal annoyed at present by bands of lawless characters roaming about, and levying blackmail on any one they are able to pounce upon. Several of the brethren have already suffered severely from this form of oppression,

Other fell on Good Ground. 599

and it was very trying for one to hear of all this without being able to help them.

On Monday the 5th, I started from Giam-cheng, and arrived at our chapel in Ka-poa-soa about mid-day. Here the infant membership roll was revised and corrected up till date ; but here, I am sorry to say, I failed in my efforts to bring about a better understanding between sister Chia and her husband. While in Ka-gi, he came and made a most dolorous complaint to me about his wife refusing to live with him, and always running away to her relatives at Ka-poa-soa. She, on the other hand, affirms that her husband has hitherto failed to provide necessary articles of furniture for his house, and that he is always blaming her when his words ought to be those of gratitude and encouragement. 'Faults on both sides,' was one's almost involuntary remark. The case is a very commonplace one, and would hardly be worthy of notice, were it not to give an opportunity for remarking that we find little domestic squabbles of this kind to be not less frequent than they are a cause of most serious hindrance to the progress of our work. The whole system of Chinese betrothals and of marriage among them, as a mere matter of arrangement, is certainly not conducive to the peace and comfort of any one's home. We shall probably make detailed reference to this whole subject at one or other of the meetings of our approaching Conference.

I had a pleasant meeting with our Hoan-a-chhan brethren on the Monday evening, and reached Taiwanfoo about mid-day on Tuesday; feeling thankful for nearly everything I had seen, and more than ever hopeful of the work throughout the County of Ka-gi. To God be all the praise!

28. *Pioneering in the Pescadores.*

TOA-SIA, 10 *August* 1886.—The Pescadores, consisting of over twenty inhabited islands, besides several islets and rocks, lie off the south-west coast of Formosa at a minimum distance of about twenty-five miles, the entire group being set down on the charts as extending from latitude 23° 12′ to 23° 47′ N., and from longitude 119° 19′ to 119° 41′ E. They form together the Dashing-Lake County or *Ting* of the Taiwan (Formosa) Prefecture, and are placed under the control of resident civil and military mandarins, who report to their superior officers at Taiwanfoo.

According to surveys made by the late

Captain Collinson, R.N., the largest island is forty-eight miles, and the second largest seventeen miles, in circumference. The former of these occupies a north-east position, and is known in native statistical works by the name of Great Island, while the latter is situated at an average distance of fully three miles west from Great Island, and is called West Island by the Chinese, and Fisher Island by Europeans.

Makeng, on the south-west end of Great Island, is the principal town of the group. It overlooks one of the inlets of the large well-sheltered harbour of the same name, and is the headquarters of a considerable junk-trade which is carried on between those islands and the west coast of Formosa.

The passage between Great Island and Fisher Island is narrowed very much at its northern end by coral reefs and by the land trending inward from both sides, and to the deep lagoon or bay thus formed the Chinese apply the name Dashing-Lake, which, as already stated, is given also to the whole county.

The other large islands are all found to the southward of Great Island ; first, Rover Channel, about six miles broad ; and then, Steeple Channel, about three miles broad, having to be crossed before any boat, leaving Makeng Harbour, can go on to Junk Island, the southernmost limit of the group.

As seen from a distance, the Pescadores present an appearance which is decidedly bleak and unimpressive. In no direction does the land rise higher than three hundred feet above the sea-level, the greater part of it being much lower even than this, of table-like flatness, and almost wholly destitute of trees and bushes.

It is only on closer inspection that the larger islands, especially, come into a more favourable light. Those bare, sandy-looking plains are then found to be under a high state of cultivation; and although, on account of strong winds, drought, and uncongenial soil, a rice-field is scarcely to be seen, this want is never felt while gazing upon those broad waving fields of Barbadoes millet. The numerous villages, too, having clean and substantially-built houses of coral with tiled roofs, add to the attractiveness of the scene; they are usually situated in snug little bays, or up some quiet little creek, where boats find at once shelter and a ready outlet to the sea.

The population of the Pescadores is stated by intelligent natives to be about eighty thousand, and there seems less difficulty in arriving at a fairly correct estimate upon this point from the fact of the inhabitants being parcelled out into so many islanders, amongst whom there is constant intercommunication, and whose circumstances are all thoroughly well known to the merchant and official classes at Makeng. The great majority of them are the descendants of settlers from the Amoy region of the Fokien Province.

Most of the farming work is done by the female portion of the people, whilst the men are usually engaged in their fishing-boats, or in conducting the extensive bartering trade between Formosa and the Pescadores; the export articles of this trade consisting chiefly of salted fish, ground-nuts, pigs, fowls, and eggs, which are given in exchange for rice, sweet-potatoes, fruit, salt, and other such commodities.

A matter for much regret is that, with the importation of those necessary articles, a large quantity of opium is also brought over. In an isolated place like this, it would not have awakened any surprise had the use of the drug been altogether unknown, but such is far from being the case, as opium is in much greater demand than it is in the fishing-villages of Western Formosa. By way of explanation, the people remarked that, occasionally, stormy weather would place them in enforced idleness for weeks at a time, and that many of them smoked opium to obtain relief from rheumatism and severe headaches.

It ought to be added that the education of the young receives an amount of encouragement here which is very gratifying. Nearly every village has its school, and I was informed that it is quite an ordinary occurrence for more than one hundred young men from the Pescadores to go up to the examinations for Chinese

Pioneering in the Pescadores. 607

degrees which are held triennially in Taiwanfoo. Graduates of the first degree are frequently to be met with, even *Ku-jin* turn in this direction to their ancestral home, while an insignificant little island is exultingly pointed out as being the birthplace of one who obtained his much coveted degree from Peking.

The Pescadores came first, prominently, under the notice of Western nations in the early part of the seventeenth century. It was in 1622 that the commanders of an expedition from *Holland* were repulsed in an attempt to establish themselves at Macao, and it was during the course of the following year that their small fleet sailed up the coast of China and took forcible possession of these islands.

The resistance offered to them must have been very slight. Trade with Formosa was still a question of the future, communication with the mainland much less frequent than it is at present, and the inhabitants of the Pescadores, then few in number, were dependent almost exclusively upon their own slender resources for sustenance and protection.

The conclusion, therefore, arrived at by the officers in charge was that it would be madness to engage in conflict with those powerful strangers, and that no alternative was left them but to submit to the humiliation of seeing the Dutch flag unfurled over what was afterwards to become the Dashing-Lake County of Taiwan.

Of course, intelligence of what had taken place was in due time conveyed to the *Yamen* of the Provincial Governor. Captain Collinson thus continues the narrative: 'The authorities of the opposite coast of Fuhkien, at Amoy and Fuhchau, unsuccessfully endeavoured to drive out the new-comers; but, finding this means futile, they urged them to leave it for the richer acquisition of Formosa. This was at first declined, but after a series of alternate negotiations and ruptures, hostile attacks and specious treaties, between the parties, very characteristic of those times, and the landing of 4000 Chinese troops to garrison a fortress on the largest island of the group, and thus prevent all trade, the Dutch agreed to move over to Formosa, where they built Fort Zeelandia. Their conduct had been so harsh towards the natives of the Pescadores, and such prisoners as they had taken while holding possession of them, that the people on the main declined to trade with them.'

One thing brought out during the course of this struggle was the very manifest preference which those early adventurers had for the Pescadores over the more fertile and immensely more extensive territory of Formosa. The reason is an apparent one: the Pescadores have abundant harbour accommodation, whereas Formosa had much better be shunned by any one attempting to escape from the treacherous currents and roaring typhoons of the China Sea.

As compared with Macao, recent experience made it somewhat natural that the Hollanders should unanimously decide in favour of the Pescadores. Here they would be only one day's sail from the mainland; here they would be within easier distance of the great northern markets; and here, above all, their insular position would secure them against daily annoyances and the fear of a sudden attack.

It has already been seen, however, that this grand scheme of the Hollanders for crippling the Portuguese, and enriching themselves by the establishment of a shipping and commercial depot on the Pescadores, was not to be realised; and the old ruined Dutch Fort on the south side of the entrance to Makeng Harbour still remains an appropriate witness to the futility and unscrupulousness of their attempt.

A long interval of fully two hundred and sixty years has to be bridged over before reaching the only other occasion when those islands became invested with anything like a national importance. One quiet afternoon during the spring of 1885, the people of Formosa were startled on hearing what seemed to them the sound of distant thunder. It was not thunder, but the ponderous ironclads of *France* engaged in demolishing the fortifications over against Fisher Island and Makeng. Those fortifications were mounted with good-sized guns of foreign make, and occupied by several thousands of soldiers who had been hastily collected from various stations on the mainland. It availed nothing; fighting was to be conducted in a style very different from that of other days; and sure enough, before long, the huge floating batteries of the French fleet loomed in sight.

According to popular report, no time was lost with any kind of preliminary formalities. The Chinese commenced to fire upon the advancing ships, which continued steadily and with ominous silence to press forward in the direction of Makeng. When within about pistol-shot range, there burst from them such a tremendous discharge against the large Fort outside of the town, that many a heart must have been filled with terror and amazement. Indeed, some say that on witnessing the fearful havoc caused by this opening volley from the French guns, both officers and men began to scamper off from the entrenchments; a statement which, however, cannot be altogether correct, since the number of soldiers suffering from frontal wounds who afterwards found their way to the Mission Hospital at Taiwanfoo shows conclusively that not a few of those poor, matter-of-fact Chinamen must have made a noble stand against the invaders of their country.

So soon as the French had taken possession of Makeng, notifications were issued to inform all whom it concerned that what was taking place arose out of a quarrel between two great nations, for which quarrel the people of those nations were in no sense responsible—that efforts had been made to shield the innocent from all kinds of needless suffering—that peacefully-disposed natives had now nothing to fear—and that, whatever might be asked from them in the form of goods or labour would willingly be paid for at the current rates.

It must have been about this time that the name of Admiral Courbet—Kok *Tai-jin*—came so much to be respected by the inhabitants of the Pescadores. Under his firm hand, anything approaching to excess on the part of the French seamen was instantly checked, and every means was taken to make it known that protection to all the rights of life and property might be depended upon, so long as the new Authority lasted and the people themselves remained quiet.

A great many of the shops and houses in Makeng had been destroyed either by shells thrown from the ships, or by retreating Chinamen who wished to leave as little as they could for the French, and who also, perhaps, wished to do some little amount of looting on their own behalf. Be this as it may, the tumble-down condition of the buildings did not prevent hundreds of those who fled at the commencement of hostilities from returning; nor did it lessen their eager desire to earn as many as possible of those good, clean, Mexican dollars which now streamed in upon the place. The French made liberal use of their services as coolies and boatmen, builders, and carpenters also finding ready employment; while the large daily supplies of fish, meat, and vegetables brought in, were purchased at prices which must have rejoiced the heart of John Chinaman himself. It speaks very much to the credit of every one that, during this more peaceful period of their relations, there was an entire absence of anything like oppression from the European side or of wanton retaliation from that of the Chinese.

Towards the close of their brief occupation, the French erected two substantial wooden jetties at Makeng. They allowed those jetties to remain when the place came to be evacuated, even although formed of excellent timber, and capable of being easily taken to pieces; they also allowed the little mortuary-chapel-looking building on the plateau, up from the town, to remain intact.

It is just a matter for sincere regret that before leaving the French did not, either selfishly or considerately, carry away with them the many unexploded shells which may still be found embedded in the earth, or lying on the open fields in the neighbourhood of Makeng. No fewer than five accidents, causing the death of at least twenty persons, have taken place through the obstinate recklessness of Chinamen who will persist in meddling with those dangerous articles. They succeeded in unfastening one of the shells and in selling the powder inside for three hundred *cash* ; but their usual method of procedure is to hurl heavy stones at them, in the hope of obtaining a larger sum for the broken pieces of metal which may afterwards be picked up. At the latest of those tragic occurrences, one young man survived the accident, but two of his companions were blown into a thousand fragments. I happened to be near the spot at the time, and called upon the District Magistrate to suggest that all the remaining shells should be carefully taken on board a fishing-boat and dropped into twenty fathoms of water. His only response was a faint smile.

Another somewhat mournful fact which may be mentioned here is suggested by the sight of the three lonely little cemeteries containing the remains of those officers and men of the French force who died from sickness or from wounds. The furthest off is situated at the foot of the low-lying hill opposite Junk Bay, the two others being on the plain up from the town, and within view of the waters of Dashing-Lake Harbour. Considering the shortness of their stay on the Pescadores, and the total number of graves to be seen, the death-roll of the French must have been a very alarming one. The Chinese themselves admit that this was not on account of the fighting, and they still speak with something approaching to genuine feeling of the frequency with which the victims of fever and cholera were carried out to their last resting-place. The walls, gates, wooden crosses, and other property connected with the three cemeteries continue to be kept in perfect condition so far as any interference from

the natives is concerned, and it was one day about the middle of last June that I stood with a large crowd looking in through the gate at an obelisk of dressed coral which loving hands have raised to the memory of Admiral Courbet. The people around me were all very obliging and communicative, and the following were some of the remarks they made about him whose Memorial stood now before us :—
' *I chin ho-ta*—he was exceedingly brave ; *I put-chi giam*—he was very strict ; *I gau the-thiap kan-kho lang*—he was good at sympathising with miserable people.' Brave, just, compassionate. What a noble testimony ! Coming also from those to whom he stood in the relationship of conqueror ! Could the ambition of any true knight reach higher ? There was at least one head uncovered in that little crowd.

It is time, however, to make some reference to the Pescadores as a field of labour for the Christian missionary. Fully half a century ago, the devoted Gutzhaff halted here on his way to Formosa, but his stay was very brief, and limited almost entirely to the distribution of tracts and copies of the Scriptures. This is the only such visit to the Pescadores of which any record has been found till the one from which I have just returned.

I left Taiwanfoo about four months ago, and after overtaking the usual amount of pastoral duty throughout Chiang-hoa, had the way opened for me to engage in some preaching-work among the more seldom visited towns and villages of our wide field. It occurred to me then that this would be the best time for carrying out a long-cherished wish to visit the

Pescadores. On mentioning the matter to Brother Tiong, he at once expressed a desire to accompany me, and we made arrangements to start from Toa-sia about the end of May.

Three days' journey in a south-westerly direction brought us to the coasting village of Tang-chioh, where we found a junk about to clear for Makeng. My application for a passage seemed to awaken very suspicious and avaricious thoughts among those on board, but after much jangling, an agreement was come to and we went on board. I spent three most miserable days in that wretched little junk. Five of the eight sailors were opium-smokers, and their constant devotion to the pipe kept the little tank of a cabin so filled with black smoke, that it was impossible for me to remain below. Another thing was that, as we were slowly moving down the river, a heavy gale set in which held us prisoners at the mouth of the creek and often threatened to send the old craft bowling over the sand around us. The weather greatly moderated at the close of the third day, and after a rather pleasant passage of some ten hours, the boat quietly anchored in Makeng harbour on Sabbath evening the 6th of June.

We went ashore next morning, and were immediately surrounded by a large crowd of curious and interested spectators. As some rumours were in circulation that the French wished to return to the Pescadores, it caused no surprise when several messengers from the Magistrate's office arrived to inquire who I was and what was my business. We were busily engaged in selling Christian tracts when they came forward, and seemed quite satisfied when I

Pioneering in the Pescadores. 623

informed them that we came from the Church in Formosa, and wished only to 'preach the doctrine' to the people here.

After a few necessary preparations, we set out for the native village of *Lim Kiam-kim*, who was at one time tutor of our Christian college in Formosa and an earnest preacher of the Gospel, but who died in his own home a few years ago. We remained at this village of Lam-liau for two days. It contains about a thousand inhabitants, has a number of other villages in the immediate neighbourhood, and would be a most desirable centre for carrying on every branch of missionary work. Although no very marked traces of Kim's influence were met w th on the present occasion, the people seemed to entertain an unmistakably respectful feeling for the memory of our departed brother, and they certainly listened to the message now brought to them with no small degree of sustained and discriminating attention.

At our opening meeting, about three hundred persons sat till midnight as we preached to them of man's sin and of salvation through a crucified and risen Redeemer; and before separating, the numerous questions which were asked gave us most encouraging proof that our words had not been spoken in vain. On the two following days, equally good meetings were held, hundreds of Christian sheets and books were disposed of, while scores of people who kindly called upon us were spoken to more personally about the things that belong to their peace. I noticed that the children were much pleased on having front places assigned to them at our gatherings, and on a few of the elder lads being presented with neat little picture leaflets. Generally, I should say that the region here is ripe for having a preacher stationed in it. At least four persons knew something of the Gospel from missionary addresses they had listened to elsewhere, and through them there would be no difficulty in securing suitable Mission premises.

Our next halting-place for a short time was at Chhiah-kham, the most northerly town on Great Island, and one of the small ports which carry on trade with the fish-stores of Formosa. The people had already heard of our work in and around Lam-liau, and were so far prepared for our arrival. Probably every house in the place sent its representative to meet us that evening in the little temple-area up from the shore. No one could desire more attentive audiences; and here, too, it was midnight before they could be prevailed upon to disperse.

After visiting several other places, we engaged a little open boat. Tiong went to preach in two more villages, while I set sail for Ka-poa-su, the Bird Island of the Admiralty chart. I was very desirous to visit this island. Nearly all the numerous wrecks take place at its northern end, and several persons said that the inhabitants were most favourable to foreigners, owing to the British Consul having lately come in a man-of-war to bestow handsome rewards on some of the people for their humane treatment of shipwrecked seamen. As the boat drew near, and it was seen that the only passenger on board was a foreigner, many of the islanders turned out to learn the object of the visit. On walking up from the beach, the first intelligible sound which reached me was the voice of a man calling out, '*Bok-su! Bok-su!*'—'Pastor! Pastor!' It was indeed an answer to prayer, one of many we had been receiving during the past few days. The man who addressed me in this way had paid several visits to Taiwanfoo, and knew something of the nature of our work. Later on, I preached to the crowd which gathered, and while doing so, a sailing-boat was seen approaching, having faithful little Tiong on board, who was both able and eager to help me. We soon had before us an audience of about four hundred and fifty persons, for I roughly counted them as they sat in rows on the dry sand in front of us. Tiong's address that night was one of much power, and delivered with great warmth and tenderness.

Next day we landed on Conch Island, and remained preaching and speaking to the people there for two days. Sand Island was afterwards visited, and then we had rather a risky little voyage in crossing to begin work among the thirteen villages on Fisher Island. The opportunities presented here were both numerous and most inviting. Never can the sight of those crowds, listening with rapt attention for the first time to the words of eternal life be effaced from my memory. Some of our meetings were held under clear moonlight, but were none the less impressive on that account. Indeed, past experience convinces me that the time of full-moon during summer is one of the choicest for village-preaching in China; provided always, of course, that the matter be gone about in a right way. An important condition is that the people require to know beforehand of our being in the neighbourhood, and of our desire to meet a large company of them that evening in some well-known square or meeting-place outside. The irrepressible and ubiquitous boy-element should also be taken into ac-

Pioneering in the Pescadores. 629

count, as I have more than once lost favourable opportunities through bands of mischievous urchins calling in the aid of every village cur to the Pandemonium of sound which drove me from the place. It is better to treat with them at once, a little management being all that is needed for gaining them over as friends, or even converting them into most useful and willing allies.

At the close of a week's hard and pleasant work here, I thought it best to return to Makeng. The opening in every direction seemed so unmistakable, that I wished to obtain possession of some house that would serve as headquarters for future work, my intention also being to continue our journey to the islands of the southern or Rover group. We accordingly again hired an open boat, and after a good six hours' tossing and tacking, were able to land at the mouth of Makeng Harbour. Many were our silent prayers that God would raise up some friendly native who would help us. Of course, we knew no one. As our small *impedimenta* lay on the street, Tiong came back time after time to say that the people were afraid to show us hospitality in case they might be called to account for doing so. An elderly man then invited us into his shop, and said that the people of Makeng had all heard of our work, and were favourably disposed towards us, but fear of the Mandarins kept them under restraint, the recent bombardment of the place making them all the more afraid of incurring their displeasure. At last, a man came forward and remarked that he would accept the responsibility and try to find us a room, and in an hour after we were in our ' own hired house '—or stable, as some would have called it—receiving all that came to us, and preaching daily to the crowds which assembled outside.

It was while thus engaged I began to suffer from the coarse Chinese fare and unsuitable sleeping accommodation we had sometimes been compelled to put up with. I did not know till afterwards that the grated potatoes we made use of on Conch Island were eighteen months old and moving with worms, and here I now lay, suffering intense agony, and with no one at hand who could understand or minister to my wants. Even yet, I hardly know how I succeeded in getting on board a small Government steamer which was crossing to Amoy. Tiong remained behind, and I left empty-handed and alone.

My sickness lasted for about ten days, but as soon as possible I returned to Formosa, and travelled from Tamsui to Toa-sia, where most kind and brotherly messages were awaiting me from my colleagues at Taiwanfoo. Their letters stated that the Pescadores visit had awakened so much interest among our native brethren in the south, that they were already offering funds for beginning a permanent mission to those islands. The Toa-sia congregation had a crowded missionary meeting that evening of my arrival, at which I recounted the details of our work on the Pescadores, and informed them of the interest which the visit there had already awakened among their fellow-Christians in Taiwanfoo. At the close of my address, one of the most influential and respected of our members rose and said that surely God had been answering their prayers, that with regard to this Pescadores Mission he would only be too willing to help, were it not that those present wished

Entrance into Chiang-hoa. 633

to see something done in their own county city, and that, to begin a mission there, he was now prepared to hand over not less than thirty dollars. Thereupon, another member rose and said that he would add ten, a third promised five, and within the next forty-eight hours it was decided that the Toa-sia Church should attempt to begin a mission within the walls of the neighbouring city of Chiang-hoa.

29. *Entrance into Chiang-hoa.*

TAIWANFOO, 1 *November* 1886.—This city is one to which our longing eyes have been often turned. Its inhabitants are rather a turbulent race, and more than once have our attempts to preach to them ended in confusion and general uproar. Through the Hospital at Taiwanfoo and otherwise, some of them know about the Church, and we have often thought that stated preaching-work here would be a step in the right direction, had it only been possible to obtain some kind of place in which to meet.

The initial step of trying to secure mission premises in any of the large cities of China is nearly always attended with no small amount of difficulty, and sometimes even of danger. It has been truly said that officials and literati dislike the missionary, and easily succeed in getting the mob to oppose his work. The action of our Toa-sia brethren three months ago, in raising funds to attempt the establishment of a mission in Chiang-hoa, put the matter in a new light, and made us feel that now if ever was the time for successful action.

I happened then to be spending the summer in this region, and was only too glad to have the opportunity of lending a

Entrance into Chiang-hoa.

helping hand. Several of the native brethren accompanied me on two or three preliminary visits to the city, and as the result of our inquiries, it was found that a certain house-owner was in monetary difficulties and willing to treat with us. His property consisted of two shops in a quiet part of West Street which, with some necessary alterations, would provide ample accommodation for hospital and evangelistic work. Meanwhile, the two back rooms where we found temporary lodgement soon appeared to be a general rallying-place for all the vermin and evil smells of the neighbourhood. Will any one tell me how it is possible that human beings can live and thrive in many of those Chinese inns? Such expressions as insanitary, ill-ventilated, untidy, or unwholesome convey no description whatever of their condition, and one is puzzled to know why cholera morbus and every kind of deadly epidemic should at any time be absent from them. On this occasion, I could hardly venture out of doors, as strong opposition set in when it became known that attempts were being made to set up a 'Jesus-Church' in the city.

We began by handing over about fifty dollars as part-payment to our impecunious friend, who signed a little document which gave us a sort of *locus standi* in the case. I question if it dawned upon him then that matters would come to our actually getting into possession of his property. Chinaman-like, he grasped at the money, and trusted to the chapter of accidents for some kind of excuse that would free him from delivering up the title-deeds. The fifty dollars were squandered that day they came into his hand, the title-deeds were scattered about among relatives who had advanced money upon them, and when it was noised abroad that further sums would be forthcoming from the foreigner, a number of creditors pressed in to insist upon the payment of their debts.

At this stage the strong anti-foreign and anti-missionary opposition in the city became every day more manifest. When one of the native brethren who accompanied me went out for the daily supply of food, he was invariably recognised and followed by persons who said they would take his life. On several occasions, I was myself mobbed and jostled about in a very unpleasant way; and once while walking on the city walls, so many stones were thrown at me that I had to make a hasty descent into the street, and again find my way through a network of back lanes into our dreary little den. Shortly after this, some men of the baser sort banded themselves together and came to the inn where we lodged, with the determination of chasing us off. They burst in the main door of the front room, and commenced to threaten in a most alarming way. It was then about two in the morning, and the dark street was lighted up with torches which some of them carried. I ran out and tried to talk to them pleasantly about being away from their beds at this untimely hour, but they immediately began to shout and yell against the setting-up of any foreign church here. The excitement continued till daybreak, and one could plainly see that only the first blow was needed to have our efforts in Chiang-hoa at this time quenched in blood.

I hardly knew what to do. The old native Elder of our party was beginning to break down under the strain, while we

Entrance into Chiang-hoa. 639

all admitted that if once the position were given up, any renewal of the attempt to gain a foothold in Chiang-hoa would be well-nigh impossible. Many were the prayers we offered that God would open up the way before us, but everything seemed dark and unpromising, and it was with very little hope of success that I at last made up my mind to call on the County Magistrate, to see if he would not interpose and have the transaction completed in our favour. At most, I thought he would only do as others in his position have repeatedly done before, namely, give a polite promise to inquire into the case, and afterwards report that there were insuperable difficulties in the way of giving us a legal title to the property. I first sent my Chinese card with a request that the attendants at the *Yamen* would take it in, but they said that His Honour was busy; another card brought the reply that he was asleep, and a third they refused to accept. I thereupon marched down the street, passed through an excited crowd into the main gate of the *Yamen*, crossed the first and second court inside, and then stood at the door of His Honour's own private apartment. He must have seen me coming forward, for I noticed him darting into an inner room and hastily fastening his official robe about him. When he did appear, I had a feeling of almost inexpressible relief and astonishment to find that he was a man I met eight years before under very different circumstances.

A correct understanding of the position can be obtained only by making a short digression here. In 1878, I travelled down through the Heng-chhun county to visit several of the aboriginal tribes in that

Entrance into Chiang-hoa. 641

region. While at South Cape then, I found the people and some officials in a state of considerable excitement over what was said to be the wreck and plunder of an American ship. The inquiries made led me to think that there was something very unaccountable about the conduct of the men who were in charge of this ship. She was run into Kwaliang Bay one evening, and when natives put off from the shore to ask what was wanted, muskets were levelled at them by those on board, and all attempts at communication peremptorily forbidden. On a messenger informing the District Magistrate of the circumstance, officers came down and were rowed out, but only to meet with a similar repulse. Just before dark, another ship made its appearance in this rarely-visited spot, and anchored about three hundred yards from the first

2 S

one. Apparently every man on board the first ship then hurriedly left in a small boat to the second, and had no sooner done so, than the former blew up with a loud explosion. From the expectant attitude of those in the little boat and on board the second ship, it was quite evident that what took place was a pre-arranged affair.

After paying a visit to the Ku-a-lut savages at that time, I came north again, crossed over to Lombay Island, and then continued my journey up to Takow. On reaching the Port, I was a good deal surprised to see indications of unusual stir in the neighbourhood. Three large men-of-war were anchored outside. I never met here with so many naval officers and blue-jackets, while long-robed Chinamen with military attendants appeared to have quite taken possession of the place. I had scarcely reached the Mission House before the British Consul informed me that a ship named the *Forest Belle* had been wrecked and plundered of a valuable cargo at South Cape, and that the Court now being held was dealing with the American captain's claim for enormous damages from the Chinese Government. I don't know what made me do so, but at that moment two things came into my mind, the first being a recollection of the fact that China had lately paid half a million of *Taels* to the Japanese under somewhat similar circumstances, and the second, that there seemed something exceedingly queer about the proceedings of this American compatriot.

Mr. H. E. Hobson, the Commissioner of the Imperial Customs, was also on the alert that day, and no sooner heard of my arrival from this remote part of the Island than he obtained from me all I could say about the one unvarying story of the *two* ships, the cargo of *coal* in the one which was destroyed, the wreckage washed ashore, and the activity of the local officials in trying to render every helpful service they could. In short, I attended the Court upon the invitation of His Excellency *Ha To-tai*, and among all the Chinese officers who were present, none gave me a more joyful welcome than the Magistrate in whose district the alleged wreck and robbery took place, the result of the whole being that my statement had at least some share in leading to the apprehension and imprisonment of the American captain for wilful fraud.

This Heng-chhun magistrate, then, was the same man before whom I now stood in the Chiang-hoa *Yamen*. He had been promoted about a year before, and was

Entrance into Chiang-hoa. 645

now administering the affairs of this much larger county. He was somewhat stiff when I entered, but no sooner had I called to his recollection the circumstances under which we met eight years before, than his manner and very appearance completely changed. He at once took me by the arm, led me into his private room, had fruit and tea brought in, and then asked what he could do for me. I told him about the difficulty we were experiencing with a certain landlord in the city; that this man had already received our money for the lease of his house, but seemed either unable or unwilling to carry out his part of the agreement. The magistrate then and there ordered two *Yamen*-runners to go and have the man brought before him, and meanwhile he chatted with me about all sorts of subjects. When our needy friend arrived, His Honour very impressively told him that if he did not instantly take steps to implement his part of the bargain, he would be most severely dealt with. Poor fellow! I was truly sorry for him, he was in such a condition of abject terror.

I then rose and was about to thank the magistrate before leaving, but he came out and accompanied me down the middle of the inner court, the two great folding-doors in front of us being opened, and the large crowd in the outer court giving way as we walked down to the main entrance. Here, in presence of hundreds, he parted from me in the most cordial and polite way. There can be no doubt that the news of this favour spreading immediately through the city did much to alter our position in the eyes of many. Indeed, we were afterwards informed that the magistrate remarked to those around him

Entrance into Chiang-hoa. 647

that I was an old friend of his, that I had rendered good service eight years ago, and that he would not allow me to be molested.

Although this interview and the knowledge of it virtually settled the case, we had an immense amount of trouble in getting into actual possession of the premises. I had to see the magistrate on two subsequent occasions, being treated with the same kindness and respect as before. At the last interview, he told me he was soon removing to another county, and would be replaced by that officer before whom I appeared half-naked one morning about twelve years ago, after running away from the chapel-burning at Peh-tsui-khe.

The last item in this narrative is, that the magistrate, to whom under God we are indebted for our present foothold in this anti-foreign heathen city of Chiang-hoa, now lies in his *Yamen—a corpse.* The chapel premises had just been secured, and there were still a number of details to settle, when this tall, active officer, of about forty-five years of age, suddenly took trouble and died.

Our opening meeting here yesterday, when the place was filled with willing listeners, was an occasion of much rejoicing. We had all along tried to act in a straightforward, patient, and forgiving way with this people, and the result is that many of them seem to be really well-disposed toward us. The work now commenced among them is no doubt still a very small one; but, whether as regards the action of the Toa-sia Church in providing the necessary funds for it, or the fact that our residence within the city is now made legally secure we feel profoundly thankful, and very hopeful for

Entrance into Chiang-hoa. 649

the future. My Chinese friends may think that I am taking a rather strange way of showing this to-night. I have not seen a European face for nearly four months, and am preparing to start to-morrow at daybreak for Po-sia, but felt it impossible to leave the city without repeatedly singing out a Psalm which has now become so closely associated in my mind with the 'Battle of Chiang-hoa,' that I shall here write down every word of it :—

>   Now Israel
>   may say, and that truly,
>   If that the Lord
>   had not our cause maintain'd ;
>   If that the Lord
>   had not our right sustain'd,
>   When cruel men
>   against us furiously
>   Rose up in wrath,
>   to make of us their prey ;
>
>   Then certainly
>   they had devour'd us all,
>   And swallow'd quick,
>   for aught that we could deem ;

Such was their rage,
    as we might well esteem.
And as fierce floods
    before them all things drown,
So had they brought
    our soul to death quite down.

The raging streams,
    with their proud swelling waves,
Had then our soul
    o'erwhelmed in the deep.
But bless'd be God,
    who doth us safely keep,
And hath not giv'n
    us for a living prey
Unto their teeth,
    and bloody cruelty.

Ev'n as a bird
    out of the fowler's snare
Escapes away,
    so is our soul set free :
Broke are their nets,
    and thus escaped we.
Therefore our help
    is in the Lord's great name,
Who heav'n and earth
    by His great pow'r did frame.

30. Work for the Blind.

AYR, 24 *April* 1889.—I feel thankful that my second furlough now has given me the opportunity to prepare several embossed books for the blind in Formosa, and a few notes on this subject may not be without interest to other missionary brethren who have been somewhat similarly engaged.

It is about seven years since I began to attempt a little work for this class of sufferers, but pressure of other duties kept me from giving much attention to it till the summer of 1884. I happened then to be visiting our congregation at Giamcheng, and had a blind man introduced to me who wished to be examined for baptism. His eye-sockets were empty, and one could see at a glance that he was an intelligent man of some little character.

He accounted for his blindness by saying that over ten years ago he was going along a quiet country road in this neighbourhood, when five or six men stepped from behind a hedge, dragged him to the ground, and left him soon after with both his eyes gouged out. He added that the followers of Gaw-chi-ko and other wicked men had served about a hundred persons in the same way.

Of course, the man's statement made a very deep impression upon me, and the version of it which was sent home seemed also to awaken a considerable amount of interest, this being especially the case with a daughter of that Mr. John Alston of Glasgow who prepared the first complete edition of the Scriptures in any language for the use of blind readers. Those sympathising friends saw the opportunity, wished to be supplied with information regarding

Work for the Blind. 653

the probable number and condition of the blind in China, and expressed great willingness to assist in whatever well-considered effort might be made on their behalf.

It goes for the saying that the number of blind people in China must reach an enormously higher ratio than can be found in this country. The Director of the Institution for the Blind at Cairo estimates that about ten per cent. of the population there are totally or partially blind; and it is all but certain that full inquiry would reveal a somewhat analogous state of things in most parts of China. In thinking of the extent to which the Chinese suffer from small-pox and from their own uncleanly habits, one cannot be surprised that crowds of blind persons are sometimes met with in the larger cities, and that cases of ophthalmia bulk so largely in the Hospital Reports which are issued from year to year. I would be quite prepared for the statement, if accurate Census-returns reported the presence of 25,000 blind persons in Formosa and the southern half of the Province of Fokien, it being over this region that books in the Amoy vernacular form of the language are available.

So far as my inquiries have gone, the blind in China seem to be mostly engaged as beggars or as fortune-tellers. Some gain a living at pounding rice, or in treading the water-wheels which are used for purposes of irrigation, and I know one man who supports himself by making and repairing baskets. I think the beggars are the most numerous class, and their lot is certainly a very unenviable one. What makes it all the more trying is the fact that by far the greater number have been deprived of eyesight in middle life. Of 30,000 blind in England, it has been ascertained that about nine-tenths became so above the age of twenty-one. The same thing holds good in China, and a due consideration of this fact by those who attempt to benefit them would save a great amount of confusion and misdirected effort.

As education must form an important item in trying to improve the condition of this class, I began by making inquiries into the various kinds of embossed writing made use of in Europe and America. It is while doing so, that one comes first to be aware of the many different systems which have been devised for the use of the blind, and of the ungenerous way in which one particular method is oftentimes pushed forward at the expense of another. The earliest and most obvious way of enabling the blind to read was simply by embossing ordinary Roman letters, either in capitals throughout, or in capitals combined with small letters. Books in this form are still extensively used in the American institutions; and at home here, it seems open to question if there has not been a too hasty and a too general abandonment of this method. Many other embossed books have been printed in letters like the Roman, only simplified as much as possible so as to leave them more clear and open to the touch. The letters devised by Dr. Moon of Brighton fall under this head, and the embossed literature created by him has been of priceless value in the education of the blind. A third group of alphabets is made up of purely arbitrary signs, and of these, the dot-system of Braille seems destined to supersede all others.

Work for the Blind. 657

In coming to a decision as to the most suitable instrument for our purpose in Formosa, several things had to be taken into account, which could only occur to one having a local and technical knowledge of the position. For example, the form of the language in use here enjoys the unique privilege in China of possessing the entire Scriptures translated into ordinary Roman letters. Many other books have been prepared in this form, and the literature is rapidly increasing. Thus, by using the same Bible in Formosa and throughout the Chin-chew and Chang-chew prefectures on the mainland, we come to have hundreds upon hundreds of people scattered over a very wide region who are perfectly familiar with this simple alphabetic way of spelling out the native sounds. Another thing is that not more than nineteen letters of the English alphabet, with four tonal marks, suffice for writing out every short monosyllabic word of the spoken language, none of our books in the Romanised colloquial form containing any of the following letters: *d, f, q, r, v, w, x, y, z.*

In short, I decided to begin by having several books prepared in raised block letters, and only with such modifications as would still leave them recognisable by the sighted-readers of our Romanised Bible. Dr. Moon's system would have been adopted in its entirety, were it not that the great difference of being able to dispense with no fewer than nine of his letters, made it possible to bring several of the others into somewhat nearer resemblance to the ordinary English form. One instance of this is in the letter T, of which Moon uses only the upper horizontal bar, and in E, where he removes the two lower ones; whereas the only change I have made on both letters, is the omission of the short middle bar from the latter. Further, it seemed to me that at the present stage it would be a greater gain to the many scattered blind people were Moon's return-line arrangement eliminated, and all the lines made to read with a *forward* motion. Those familiar with the Moon books are aware that the lines read alternately from left to right and from right to left, thus enabling the reader to continue without lifting the finger. Of course, this method raises the question as to how the letters in every return line should be placed, whether reversed, or allowed to remain in their own *absolute* position. Constant practice makes either way simple enough, but there can be no doubt that this return-line arrangement introduces a certain amount of confusion, and certainly lessens the number of those sighted-readers who can render continual service to the blind.

The books which have been prepared include (1) a Primer; (2) a Reading Book; (3) the Gospel of St. Matthew in two volumes—printed by the liberality of the British and Foreign Bible Society; and (4) an edition of the *Biau-chiok Bun-tap*, or, Conversations between Evangelist and a Chinese Temple-keeper, in which Christian life is compared with the beliefs and practices of the heathen. The type has been made purposely large, being similar in size to the ordinary Moon letters. No difficulty is experienced in getting the Chinese to understand the system, and, without any additional agency, it is now possible to send books into places seldom or never visited by the missionary, which become at once available for the instruction of the blind. It may be added here, however, that it is not intended to provide an extensive supply of books in this particular form. It was a necessary condition to provide some, or almost entirely overlook the wants of thousands of isolated and hard-handed adults, to whom every complicated system would be useless, and who must be dependent on the assistance of our sighted readers.

Arrangements are now in progress to have books prepared also in Braille, by using his dots to represent the nineteen alphabetic forms and combining these phonetically, as we do with the letters in our Romanised colloquial books. It is beyond all question that the Braille system is superior to every other for educational purposes. The fact that it can be written so easily is an enormous gain, and the comparatively moderate size and price of books prepared according to it should not be overlooked. A copy of Moon's Bible requires sixty-two large volumes, and cannot be produced under ten pounds sterling, while the same work in Braille can be put into forty-nine volumes at half the cost. And yet, by those who are best qualified to form an opinion on the subject, it would be an untold calamity to the great majority of the blind themselves were this system the only one in use. Its true place seems to be the schoolroom, and to meet the wants of the comparatively small number of the intelligent young amongst the blind.

On this point I prefer to cite the evidence of those who have had opportunity for making the fullest investigation. The late Miss E. Gilbert—a daughter of the Bishop of Chichester—was blind from the third year of her age, and acquired a knowledge of all the embossed alphabets, and it

Work for the Blind. 663

was after spending a lifetime in practical work among the blind in London that she thought the Braille system to be unsuited for adults whose hands have become hardened by manual labour ; that is, for about three-fourths of the blind. (*Vide* '*Elizabeth Gilbert and her Work for the Blind.*' Macmillan & Co.) Again, Dr. T. R. Armitage, of the British and Foreign Blind Association, says : ' *Two* systems are necessary to the blind—Moon's for the hard-handed, and for those who have no wish for higher intellectual culture, and Braille for the young and intelligent of *all ages*. Moon's system has qualities which make it very generally useful. It is fully spelt, and consequently can be used for primary education ; and, at the same time, in their present size, the letters can be felt by the dull, the aged, and by those whose touch has been impaired by rough work, while the approach of many of his characters to the shape of the corresponding Roman letters makes the first step more easy. It is much to be regretted, however, that along with these obvious merits there are also some serious defects. Many letters are perfectly arbitrary; and though in some cases this could not have been avoided, yet in others a closer adherence to the Roman letter would have been possible. The non-reversal of the letters in the return-line is a serious defect, and the absence of a sign to indicate a divided word at the end of a line is inconvenient.' It is still on the same important subject that an experienced educationalist among the blind expresses himself as follows: ' No one who is thoroughly conversant with the subject can doubt that, sooner or later, Braille and Moon are destined to supersede all other existing systems,—the former specially for educational purposes, and the latter for the great majority of the adult blind. Each having its own special sphere of usefulness, and both being absolutely necessary to meet the requirements of the blind, there can be no rivalry between them, nor any need for attempting to extol the merits of the one at the expense of the other.'

But I must draw these notes to a close. It would have been interesting to say a little about those branches of occupation at which this class of sufferers might earn a living for themselves. I believe that till the dawn of a far-off day, this should be the main concern with workers for the blind in China, and not the question as to how they can turn out a few expert writers or musicians. There is a danger in being too ambitious and all-embracing. Access to the Gospels, or to the Book of Psalms, would be like opening up a new world to many of our blind Church members whose wants in this direction will always be very moderate. I confess I should feel deeply thankful if we had a work going on in Formosa like that of the Outdoor Mission to the Blind in the West of Scotland. There is certainly much need for it, and its quiet steady progress would immensely help forward all our other operations.

One is sometimes led to think that the Christianity we bring to China has so much of the didactic and hortatory about it, that every opportunity for presenting its sympathetic and practical side should eagerly be taken advantage of. There is something very suggestive in the statement that Jesus *touched* the leper, that He *touched* the blind man's eyes, the tongue of the dumb, the ear of the deaf, the poor woman in fever, and the bier of the young man who was carried out of Nain. In each case He could have spoken the word only, but we should then have known something less of the self-denial and the tender compassion of our **Great Example**.

THE END.

INDEX

TO NOTES OF

RECENT WORK IN FORMOSA.

			PAGE
1. First Impressions,	.	Vol. i.	215
2. Visiting the Out-Stations,	.		228
3. Times of Refreshing,	.		241
4. Among the Sek-hoan,	.		250
5. Itinerating in the North,			278

6. More about the Sek-hoan,	Vol. ii.	331
7. Confirming the Churches,	.	344
8. The Japanese Trouble,	. .	363
9. A Narrow Escape, .	.	371
10. Another North Journey, .		388
11. Murder of Un Ong, .	.	412
12. Sons of the Prophets,	.	420
13. With Brother Pa, . .	. .	428

			PAGE
14.	Baksa New Chapel,	Vol. ii.	434
15.	Our Hakka Brethren,		441
16.	Carnival at Ka-gi,		447
17.	Evangelising in Sinkang,		456
18.	The Highways and Hedges,		465
19.	A Visit to the Ka-le,		475
20.	Declension at Tek-a-kha,		503
21.	The Canadian Mission,		517
22.	In Memoriam,		534
23.	A Christian Conference,		543
24.	Interruption from the French,		551
25.	Happy Days at Amoy,		562
26.	After the Blockade,		580
27.	Other fell on Good Ground,		585
28.	Pioneering in the Pescadores,		601
29.	Entrance into Chiang-hoa,		633
30.	Work for the Blind,		651

www.ingramcontent.com/pod-product-compliance
Lightning Source LLC
Chambersburg PA
CBHW032047220426
43664CB00008B/895